P9-CRQ-747

THE
EQUIPPER'S
GUIDE to
EVERY-MEMBER
MINISTRY

EIGHT WAYS ORDINARY PEOPLE CAN DO THE WORK OF THE CHURCH

R. Paul Stevens

foreword by J. I. Packer

WITH CONTRIBUTIONS FROM
MICHAEL GREEN & DAN WILLIAMS

INTERVARSITY PRESS
DOWNERS GROVE, ILLINOIS 60515

© *1992 by R. Paul Stevens*

All rights reserved. No part of this book may be reproduced in any form without written permission from InterVarsity Press, P.O. Box 1400, Downers Grove, Illinois 60515.

InterVarsity Press is the book-publishing division of InterVarsity Christian Fellowship, a student movement active on campus at hundreds of universities, colleges and schools of nursing in the United States of America, and a member movement of the International Fellowship of Evangelical Students. For information about local and regional activities, write Public Relations Dept., InterVarsity Christian Fellowship, 6400 Schroeder Rd., P.O. Box 7895, Madison, WI 53707-7895.

All Scripture quotations, unless otherwise indicated, are taken from the HOLY BIBLE, NEW INTERNATIONAL VERSION. Copyright © *1973, 1978, 1984 International Bible Society. Used by permission of Zondervan Publishing House. All rights reserved.*

Chapter six copyright ©*1992 by Michael Green. Used by permission.*

Cover illustration: Merilee Harald Pilz

ISBN 0-8308-1337-3

Printed in the United States of America

Library of Congress Cataloging-in-Publication Data
Stevens, R. Paul, 1937-
   The equipper's guide to every-member ministry: eight ways laity
can do the work of the church/by R. Paul Stevens.
        p.   cm.
   Includes bibliographical references.
   ISBN 0-8308-1337-3
   1. Lay ministry.   I. Title.
BV4400.S74   1992
253—dc20   *92-8750*
                                                             CIP

15	14	13	12	11	10	9	8	7	6	5	4	3	2	1
04	03	02	01	00	99	98	97	96	95	94	93	92		

Foreword   7

Introduction: That Gracious Conspiracy   9

1 Bible Learners & Lay Preachers   19

2 Small Group Leaders   37

3 Lay Pastors & Care-Givers   55

4 Worship Leaders & Gift-Brokers   75

5 Worker-Priests in the Marketplace   91

6 Neighborhood Evangelists   113

7 Skilled Marriage Builders   127

8 Justice-Workers in Society   141

Epilog   161

Appendixes   167

Notes   186

Bibliography   194

86134

Foreword

For counseling people with relational difficulties, family systems therapy is currently "in," and seems bound to remain so. The insight that dysfunctional individuals embody, reflect and carry forward the dysfunctioning of the families that produced them is so obvious that once you see it you wonder how anyone could ever have missed it. Recognition that for such individuals recovery involves facing up to what was wrong with the family, and deliberately negating that wrongness, is nowadays virtually universal. It is a great step forward.

A parallel truth is currently being grasped with regard to Christian congregations. As leaders scratch their heads and shed their tears over the inertness of "God's frozen people" so far as any conscious ministry is concerned, they are coming to see that this inertia in God's family, like any family neurosis, is historic and systemic.

In the far-off days when maintaining inherited social distinctions was seen as a virtue contributing to a stable community, it was thought proper and indeed mandatory that nonclergy should not intrude into what the clergy do. A sweet if faded children's hymn of 1848, "All Things Bright and Beautiful," celebrating "How great is God Almighty,/ Who has made all things well," contains a verse, rarely sung nowadays, that runs:

The rich man in his castle,
   The poor man at his gate,
God made them, high or lowly,
   And ordered their estate.

To which the parodist inside me, who is always trying to get out, pops
up with the ecclesiastical equivalent:

The preacher in the pulpit,
    The layman in the pew,
God made them very different,
    And keeps them that way, too.

Both sentiments did in fact have their place in the mainstream Christian
mind of 1848.

But, just as society has been right to stop thinking that God plans
permanent poverty for everyone born poor, so the church is now right to
stop thinking that God plans permanent passivity for anyone born again
in Christ. Every Christian is called to the ministry; everyone is divinely
equipped to fulfill some serving role. We are beginning to catch up with
Paul, who nearly two thousand years ago wrote that Christ from his
throne gives "some to be pastors and teachers, to prepare God's people
for works of service, so that the body of Christ may be built up . . . as
each part does its work" (Eph 4:11-16). Paul's vision of every-member
ministry in the body of Christ through the exercise of God-given gifts
was lost, it seems, soon after his time, then reappropriated by the Christian Brethren a century and a half ago, and is now dawning upon the
entire Christian community through the worldwide charismatic renewal.
This alone, leaving everything else aside, makes the present—for me, at
any rate—a good time to be alive.

In the following pages Paul Stevens, with guest writers Dan Williams
and Michael Green, all three my colleagues at Regent College, address
aspects of the new task that this new situation lays on leaders, namely the
preparing of all God's people to fulfill their ministry both inside and outside the church. In a brisk, picturesque, pleasantly anecdotal and thoroughly practical style, they deploy a fascinating mix of experience-tested material. Their book is not a treatise, trying to say the last word on some
theological question; it is really a training manual, which it is a pleasure
to commend to leaders at all levels who take their training task seriously.
So please read on—and then do something about what you have read.

J. I. Packer
Sangwoo Youtong Chee Professor of Theology
Regent College
Vancouver, B.C.

Introduction
That Gracious Conspiracy

*The first duty of the layman
in his local church is to be a nuisance.[1]*
Mark Gibbs and T. Ralph Martin

"Will the real minister please stand!" The pastor announced his sermon title at the beginning of a series designed to raise consciousness for every-member ministry. What he had not counted on was someone answering his rhetorical question. Seven people stood.

"Why did you stand?" the pastor asked. He had intended to be making his first point by now. Instead he was in a real dialog as he investigated the truly extraordinary sense of dignity in lay ministry shared by the seven. Eventually he did preach the sermon and, at the end, invited the seven to stand again to be commissioned to their lay ministry. They did, but then from the back came a shout, "Why can't the rest of us get in on it too?" So the whole congregation stood for commissioning to the work of the ministry.[2]

Would that releasing the full potential of the church were as simple as this true story!

In fact it can only happen when *all* the laity—the clergy laity and the nonclergy laity—undertake a gracious conspiracy whereby each frees the other from the entrapments of institutional Christianity. The Greek word for laity, *laos,* means the people of God. It is an incredible compliment, not a reference to second-class people or amateurs. The clergy-lay distinction was neither in the mind of the apostles nor of Jesus. People and pastor together are the laity of God. We are members of Christ and therefore bound together fiber, sinew, tissue and nerves, "held together by every supporting ligament" (Eph 4:16). Clergy-laity and nonclergy-laity are willy-nilly interdependent. Each is the other's "thou," to use Martin Buber's phrase, in the I-Thou relationships that comprise the body of Christ. Laity and clergy-laity belong to the same shirt and need to be well connected. If the first button gets done up wrongly all the others will be out of kilter.

Some pastors or Christian educators reading this might say to themselves, "I really don't feel trapped by my role. I love the ministry and I think I'm good at it." All well and good, but the New Testament presses the question, As a church leader are you investing and deporting yourself not for your own excellence in ministry, but for the excellence of every member of your church?

Or perhaps a nonclergy layperson reading this thinks, "I'm really quite happy to come to church and to be fed by my pastor. I appreciate his ministry, and I'm glad to assist him in any way I can." But, Mr., Ms. or Mrs. Layperson, I ask on the authority of the New Testament, Have you forgotten who you are? You are a minister of Jesus Christ, a holy priest, an ambassador for Christ, an agent of reconciliation in the world, salt and light and yeast. You cannot *assist* your pastor. His job is to assist *you* in your ministry!

Happily, equipping the whole people of God is now a felt need for many pastors! But it is not a need easily satisfied.

Laypersons may also be tempted to seize pastors by the throat in a nice Christian way and demand the pastors' position, or make their pastor feel guilty for having gone to seminary, for attending ministerials and conferences. But think of your pastor (if you have one). That person, if serious at all about the Christian life, is no more hungry for power, prestige and position than you are. You may stop speaking of your pastor as "the" minister, but the pastor has been put there by a hundred expectations, cues and complaints that tell your pastor every day to be different, to be available, to be omnicompetent, to be *the* minister.

For your pastor reading this book *could* mean adding yet one more burden. In addition to the impossible role of a one-person ecclesiastical band leader of the church, which most members *want,* is the further burden of being an equipper. Now the pastor must facilitate the gifts of all the members because an enlightened minority in the church demands it. Already stretched to the breaking point, the pastor cannot just keep adding renewal movements one on top of the other like a layer cake, until the cake falls over.

For the sincere pastor, ministry is never just a job. Therefore the pastor usually invests in ministry, emotionally and personally, the combination of what nonprofessionals invest in work and their discretionary time spent in the church. People say to their pastor, "You're working too hard," but they also say, "I know you are busy, *but.* . . ." It is all too easy to attach identity to such a demanding and fulfilling expression of Christian vocation. All the eggs, so to speak, are in a single basket, unless the pastor sees family as a higher priority. Then, if a crack appears in the pastor's marriage or the teen years of parenting are embarrassingly stressful, the pastor has nothing but ministry, and even that is called into question.

This didn't just happen overnight. A complex series of forces— inner, outer, social, cultural and ecclesiastical—got us to where we are, and it won't solve any equipping bottleneck to say to the pastor, "Pastor, move over and make room for me." Or the pastor to say to the layperson, "Friend, come up higher."

Misunderstanding the Equipping Task
Equipping is not delegating. Pastors think they are equipping the laity when they delegate certain parts of their ministry to laypersons. For example, a pastor may not personally enjoy doing premarital counseling, so he may train several couples in his church to gain competence and confidence in spending five or six counseling evenings with a couple before marriage (one married couple with each marrying couple). In so "equipping" lay counseling couples, the pastor may feel he has delegated some of *his* ministry to laypersons and has helped him-

self immensely. Perhaps he now has more evenings free for his own marriage and family, a laudable result!

Such training would be a good thing to do, and I am involved in training such couples on a citywide basis. But there is a better reason to do it than the fact that every church has more ministry than one person can perform: This ministry is not *the pastor's* to give away but *theirs* by right.

This truth has been underscored by the biblical teaching on spiritual gifts. The plurality, really the *plērōma* (fullness), of ministry gifts given to the body means that each member has a fraction of the ministry of Christ, like one color of the full spectrum comprising white light. Every color is needed to express the light of Christ to the world. It is ineffective for me as a pastor to function in a ministry for which God has not equipped or called me. And it is *wrong* for me to deny others the opportunity to exercise their gifts and ministry because I insist on doing it myself.

Scratching Where It Itches

It is more important to scratch where it itches than where the medical textbook says there is a concentration of nerve endings. For the serious layperson the nerve is the feeling of *underemployment*. In the church the layperson is given "busy" work. The best positions open are largely administrative jobs or committee work, tasks which Kenneth Van Wyk's research shows the local church effectively employs large numbers of willing and unwilling lay ministers.[3] But the *real* work of ministry is done by the pastor who is called with a special call, ordained, given a title and a role of great respect, sometimes out of all proportion to the character behind the office.

If the layman itches at being underemployed, the pastor itches at being *overemployed*. All too often the pastor is expected to be a one-person ecclesiastical band—preacher, pastor, counselor, evangelist, administrator and office boy. Pastors, when they are charged with such omnicompetent roles in induction services and ordination services, should run out of the church screaming. Sadly, they never do, and as unwitting accomplices both lay and clerical members hold the person to a vow that cannot possibly be kept. One person can never be *the* minister of the church and every honest minister knows this. So a book on equipping ought to touch pastor and people at the mutual intersection of their needs: the one needing help, the other needing to get more involved. But it is not that simple. I am sure if it were, equipping the saints for the work of the ministry would be as easy as falling off a log. But there is much more to equipping than merely spreading the work around a little better. The structure and environment of the church must be radically altered. These are themes we will take up. We will need to reread the New Testament on the subject of ministry and leadership as though we had never read it before. That could be exquisitely exciting or intensely upsetting.

The average layperson, for instance, is not a lazy, reluctant church member who, because of a greater interest in golf, television or the stock market, must be badgered into service. Many centuries of bad teaching and a nonliberating church environment have taught laypersons to think that their role is *not as significant as the pastor's.* In biblical truth, the layperson's ministry is *more* important where it really counts—in the world. The idea that the nonprofessional is a "layman," someone uneducated and unskilled, comes from the world not the Bible. *Layperson* in the Bible is a term of incredible honor. Again, the Greek word *laos* means the people. Once, Peter said (1 Pet 2:9-10), we were not a laity. Before Christ saved us, we were homeless waifs in the universe—without dignity, without an identity, without a future. But now we are the people of God. So a pastor can never rise to a higher position in the universe than being a layperson! That is the needed shift in the pastor's self-concept.

The layperson (in the old sense) needs to make a major shift in self-concept too. This shift will need to be reinforced by everything that is said and done, verbally and nonverbally, when God's people meet. One sermon on "every-person ministry" will not do the trick. As we will see, the problem and the solution are systemic. Be patient, then, pastor, with the rest of the laypersons!

Packaging the Saints
It is apparent that the idea of "equipping" is catching on a little. That warms the cockles of my heart. People are beginning to view the

church through equipping eyes, to see the church less like a bus (with one busy driver and many drowsy passengers) and more like a body (with all members active and essential).[4] There are some reasons for this encouraging trend: the pressure of overwork felt by pastoral leaders, the eruption of people movements, the addiction of our society to personal rights and self-fulfillment, and a genuine effect of the Spirit's irruption in our own day. Whatever the reasons, I welcome raised consciousness about equipping. But I can't welcome the *form* that this equipping interest takes.

A plethora of courses, videotapes, programs and manuals are now available to equip the saints. Churchmanship has been reduced to technology. Pastors, extrapolating on their seminary training, water down the cognitive, rational, skill and information courses they received in the cloistered ivory tower of the seminary and offer it to their hungry parishioners. Too often they offer stones instead of bread. Sometimes nonprofessional ministers crave and attend such programs thinking they are getting the real thing. Dr. Kenneth Van Wyk's research indicates that churches with low lay involvement in Christian service registered poorly in most components of equipping methods *except courses that pass information from one person to another.*[5] There are better methods, such as apprenticeship, situational learning, small group learning, but no method by itself is large enough to embrace the equipping task.[6] Most how-to courses ignore the truth that the church is the body of Christ, not a club of Christians waiting to be trained. So a more organic approach is needed.

Equipping is like being a genetic counselor because one is trying to unpack the implications of the constitutional makeup of the body of Christ. Equipping is like being an environmental engineer because a fully liberated lay ministry is "caught" in the environment of a local church not "taught" in a school. Again, it is not enough for the pastor alone *or* the laity alone to get converted to a fully liberated lay ministry. Pastors and people must work together in a gracious conspiracy of mutual respect to find out how *each* can be the other's "thou" in the full release of ministry.

The first four chapters of this book explore how and why this can be done in the gathered life of the church. Chapter one explores the subject of Bible learners and lay preachers. Chapter two, written by my colleague Dan Williams, examines the strategic importance of equipping small group leaders. The third chapter looks at the challenge of equipping lay pastors and caregivers. We conclude part one with a chapter on equipping worship leaders. But it would be a serious error to stop with these "in-house" equipping challenges.

Releasing the Church from Itself

The real work of God is done by the church in the world. The church, as William Temple once said, is the one institution that exists for those who are not its members. It does not have a mission; it *is* one. Mission comes from the heart of God, not from the need of the world. Ray Anderson states it this way: "The on-going ministry of Jesus Christ gives both content and direction to the Church in its ministry. Jesus is the minister *par excellence.* He ministers to the Father *for the sake of the world,* taking the things of God and disclosing them faithfully to sinners, and taking sinners to himself and binding them graciously into his own Sonship to the Father." [italics mine][7] Jesus said, "As the Father has sent me, I am sending you" (Jn 20:21). The sender, the sent and the sending of the church conform completely to the sender, the sent and the sending of Jesus. Our goal is not to become the body beautiful but to be the body given for the world as we share Jesus' ministry, death and resurrection.[8]

The layperson is placed strategically by God in society. As Hendrik Kraemer said in his watershed *Theology of the Laity,* "The laity is God's daily projection into the world."[9] The church can never be a building on a corner. It is like the rhythm of the blood gathering for cleansing and oxygenation in the heart and lungs *in order* to be pumped to the uttermost parts to fight disease and to bring nutrients. We do the church a disservice by "freezing" its life in its gathered life. We tend to assume that if members are sufficiently nurtured they will spontaneously "on the overflow" reach out to others as ambassadors of Christ's reconciliation in the world. Some research indicates the exact opposite.[10]

Nurture takes place by liberating lay leaders to embrace the mission of Jesus; it comes as a by-product of being equipped and involved in ministry.

So the last four chapters concern the life of God's people in the world. Chapter five discusses worker-priests in the marketplace. Chapter six, written by my colleague Michael Green, discusses neighborhood evangelists. Chapter seven explores how the systemic life of the church can build strong marriages and homes. Chapter eight explores the challenge of equipping justice-workers for society.

Conspiring Together

What a gracious conspiracy is needed for the liberation of the laity! Pastors for their part must freely confess they know little about equipping people to worship God in their business, homemaking, peacemaking and personal evangelism. They must gently and steadfastly insist that church members not hang around the church building too much. They should see that the church programs get stripped to the bare minimum so the saints have time to talk over the back fence with neighbors or to become involved in anti-poverty groups. They must insist that God's design is that members should not be church-tenders but missionaries.

Nonprofessional ministers in the gathered church must insist that the life, teaching and training of the church should be directed toward the marketplace, home and society rather than to the church. "The first duty of the layman in his local church," say Gibbs and Martin, "is to be a nuisance . . . in asking questions: 'Why do we do this or that in church?' " These authors develop this idea of a holy nuisance further. "The generally accepted idea that the life and activities of a congregation revolve around the minister and that it is he who determines what the members do and think has to be overturned. . . . This revolt can be carried out only by the laity."[11]

In a strangely complementary way both pastor and people need to be liberated *from* the church, from the church's consuming self-serving bias. It is not as easy as preaching a series of sermons on "Will the real minister please stand?" But it could start there. For when the pastor and people graciously conspire to find the best way to release the full potential of the church in the world, they make themselves radically available to God, who is more interested in this conspiracy than we are.

© 1986 Erik Johnson. Used by permission.

One

Bible Learners & Lay Preachers

Disobedience to God's Word needs no encouragement; it's abundant enough, thank you! Yet without intending to, local churches frequently establish patterns that actually hinder doing the Word. How is it possible, I keep wondering, for some Christians to hear two sermons a Sunday for the whole of their lives and still not know how to feed on God's Word for themselves. An enemy could not have devised a more ineffective system. I am convinced that two remedies for biblical illiteracy and unintended biblical disobedience are developing patterns for congregational Bible learning and equipping a choir of preachers. But first we must explore more deeply why Bible obedience does not take place as much as it should.

Every-Member Bible Study
The formula is deceptively simple: Expose people to more biblical

material than they can digest, do it in a context separated from real life, and emphasize Bible facts, not personal acts.

Imagine the typical situation of a new believer: He or she attends a Sunday morning Bible class studying Paul's three missionary journeys. Full of excitement from Dr. Luke's dynamic account of worldwide salvation in Jesus (but with no time to assimilate it), he enters the sanctuary for worship. The sermon is on "Speaking Covenant: The Ultimate Language of Love," part of a series on Hosea. The new believer is impressed with the need for covenant love in both his relationship with God and with his spouse. On the way out, he picks up the current copy of *Daily Light.* Using this or some other excellent plan for daily Bible study, he'll spend six brief sessions in Psalms. If he's really serious, he'll also attend a midweek Bible study/prayer group where the parables are being taught. But they won't explode in his mind either, because he's still half-thinking about what the TV evangelist said last night. He's effectively been inoculated.

In the Great Commission, Jesus calls not for teaching the Word but "teaching them to obey" (Mt 28:20). *Doing,* not *hearing,* biblical truth is the measure of biblical faith. When we encourage gathering information or even inspiration without learning to live it, we unwittingly encourage disobedience. We erect barriers against the Holy Spirit. Kierkegaard once said, "The moment I take Christianity as a doctrine and so indulge my cleverness or profundity or eloquence or imaginative powers in depicting it, people are very pleased; I am looked upon as a serious Christian. The moment I begin to express existentially what I say, and consequently bring Christianity into reality, it is just as though I had exploded existence—the scandal is there at once."[1] In an effort to bring Christianity into reality, I began twenty-five years ago to explore the concept of an integrated congregational curriculum.

A Congregational Learning Curriculum
Why not put the Bible into the mainstream of the church's life, linking personal study, group experience and Sunday teaching? I was pastoring Temple Baptist Church in inner-city Montreal, a multicultural fellowship composed of five diverse ethnic groups, when I began to experiment with the answer to this question. We wrote a lectionary

of daily readings that led us systematically through whole books of
the Bible. During the week, our church members met in homes of
their neighborhood and discussed three or four simple questions we
had mimeographed to help them apply the readings of the week. Then
on Sunday I preached from the study portion assigned for that week.
The community walked with me through a passage they had already
studied. From that experience I learned the principle of *reinforced
learning:* People are more likely to "do the doctrine" when they meet
that same word in more than one environment.

Ten years later, at West Point Grey Baptist Church in Vancouver,
British Columbia, the integrated approach took a quantum leap forward. I discovered that people learn a lasting lesson when they find
it for themselves. "Standing at the bus stop the other day," one of the
older sisters confessed to me, "I tried to remember something from all
the great sermons I've heard over thirty years. My mind went totally
blank. But I was flooded with gratitude when I recalled all the things
I'd discovered for myself in the Scriptures." So we designed a curriculum that aimed at learning rather than teaching. We'd spend eleven
weeks, for instance, in the book of Ephesians. Besides the daily Bible
readings, we would offer a weekly personal Bible study section and
a group experience.

The personal study was a series of inductive questions. Each person
would *observe* (What does it say?), *interpret* (What does it mean?) and
apply (What does it mean to me?). The notes we provided gave a
minimum of information—only what was needed to make sense of the
text. The group study each week took the same passage and applied
it to corporate life. Discussion questions helped the groups make fresh
discoveries as needs, gifts and concerns surfaced from exposure to the
Word. An optional group/relational exercise attempted to apply the
Scripture to relationships within the group. Relationships, we found,
are not only an arena of application but of illumination.

For example, after studying 1 Corinthians 12 and Romans 12, one
group genuinely experienced the truth that "those parts of the body
that seem to be weaker are indispensable, and the parts that we
think are less honorable we treat with special honor" (1 Cor 12:22-23).
They spent an entire evening focusing on one person at a time and

answering the question, "How has this person been used by God to minister to this group or to individuals?" They were amazed to find out how many ways the seemingly awkward personalities in the group had been essential to the health of everyone. The small groups became examples of faith on display, living demonstrations of biblical truth.

What a privilege it was on Sunday to teach people who had read the passage, discussed it among themselves, and encountered it corporately. Not once in twenty-five years has anyone complained of repetition of the same text. The most common criticism has been that we were moving too quickly through the Scripture. Often the Sunday sermon was based on something that surfaced in our Tuesday small group. No longer the lonely prophet descending from the mountain to deliver the Sunday message, I was now a fellow learner in the camp, sharing what God was teaching us all. We learned the meaning of 1 John 2:27—"You do not need anyone to teach you." It does not mean that pastors and teaching elders are unnecessary. Far from threatening my position, the experience actually enhanced it through a corporate anointing of the Scripture.

Thus at West Point Grey, I learned the principle of *discovery learning:* People will integrate into their lives what they've discovered for themselves. Dozens of excellent discovery Bible studies have been published by InterVarsity Press under the LifeGuide banner and by Harold Shaw as Fisherman Bible Studies. All of them assume the principle verified by countless studies in educational methodology, namely that people learn more effectively what they discover for themselves, rather than what they are told to learn. For example, one such study showed that small group work and laboratory research ranked first and second in effectiveness in a list of fifteen types of educational activities for young people while the lecture ranked fifteenth, the least effective![2] But we had a further step to take.

At Marineview Chapel, I divested myself of an additional clerical prerogative: I decided no longer to write the curriculum myself. A group of eight or nine, selected by the elders, met to discuss the upcoming texts, identifying the major themes we needed to confront, and then divided up the writing assignments. They met again to critique one another's work before one of the elders edited and took the material to the printer. Thus, our curricula were fully home-grown, uniquely aimed and rarely suitable for other congregations without radical editing.

Each year the elders selected the learning plan, which included at least one Old Testament book, one New Testament book, and a con-temporary topic such as economic lifestyle, spiritual formation, public discipleship or something current in the pilgrimage of our church. We planned one- or two-week gaps between series to give people a break from the daily readings, to give the groups a chance to do something other than Bible study, and to allow the elders to preach in response to some immediate need. This helped us avoid overprogramming and allowed us to scratch where people were itching. These homegrown curricula are not as good as the commercially published ones, but they are usually *better for our church*. The reason is not hard to find. The issues, illustrations and applications all relate to the realities of this particular people. And the people who prepare the study get the most from the curriculum.

The Explosive Power of Questions

Inductive Bible study means letting the Bible speak for itself rather than trying to find in the Bible a principle derived from somewhere else. Questions are crucial to this process. And the equipping pastor who understands the systemic life of the church knows that it is more important for a leader to ask the right questions than to give the right answers. Virginia Satir, a pioneer in systemic family therapy, said, "I am the leader of the process, not the leader of the people."[3] Crucial to the process is the involvement of people in owning and shaping their own ministry and life in God. So the wise pastor will find in a con-gregational learning curriculum a splendid opportunity to give stra-tegic, crucial leadership without saying a word from the pulpit or chairing the official board—all by asking the right questions.

Questions are explosive devices. They burrow into our minds and force us to come to terms with new realities. They expand our world views. They evoke our deepest thoughts and set us on a journey of discovery. They challenge our prejudices and assumptions. They empower us to become excited leaders rather than apathetic followers. One well-placed question can be more effective than a dozen well-honed speeches. But not all questions do this, and the equipping pastor must learn the art of question asking, especially in the process of writing Bible study guides.

Rhetorical questions are questions asked only half-heartedly because the teacher intends to supply the answer. Ironically some "study" guides are filled with rhetorical-type questions because the author has provided fill-in-the-blank-type questions on various Scriptures in order to prove a point. The truth is "rigged" so that the student discovers what the teacher wants the student to say, whether or not this is the true meaning of a text. Obviously true learning is at a minimum. In oral communication, rhetorical questions have some value in awaking interest, such as Jesus' question to the disciples, "To what can I compare this generation?" (Mt 11:16). But in a study guide, rhetorical questions have practically no usefulness.

Information questions request the student to provide answers of a factual kind. The answers are known to the teacher and must be observed by the student before the teacher, or curriculum writer, moves on. For example, Jesus asked the Pharisees and Herodians to bring a denarius to him to let him look at it. "Whose portrait is this? And whose inscription?" (Mk 12:16), questions essential to his pronouncement that they should give to Caesar what is Caesar's and to God what is God's. When writing study guides, information questions are crucial to observing what the text is actually saying. It keeps us from jumping to interpretation before we have stopped to attend to the facts.

Leading questions invite learners to supply answers from within themselves, as they relate to observed facts. These require more thought than information questions, and the questioner, or question-writer, supplies enough clues so the learner discovers the one true answer desired. For example, when questioned by the chief priests and elders about the authority by which he taught and healed, Jesus asked, "John's baptism—where did it come from? Was it from heaven, or from men?" (Mt 21:25). In this case, answering correctly would have implied their moral responsibility for not following John the

Baptist themselves. So they chose to be silent in response to the leading question Jesus asked.

Probing questions are the most profound. They are truly open-ended, and the teacher cannot predict what answer learners will give. A well-chosen probing question burrows into the subconscious mind and grows while the learner broods. It keeps a person on pilgrimage. For example, Jesus asked his disciples, "Who do you say I am?" (Mt 16:15). Why didn't Jesus tell his best friends the correct answer to this crucial question? (I just asked another probing question!) While Peter gave the "correct" answer and was affirmed by Jesus (16:17-19), it is obvious from the dialog that follows (vv. 21-28) that the disciples were not ready for a cross-bearing messiah and needed to brood more on his probing question. More than half the questions attributed to Jesus in the Gospels were of the probing kind. So the equipping pastor will make use of several kinds of questions, especially the probing ones, as part of developing a congregation Bible-learning model.

Experiencing Systemic Growth

The integrated curriculum is not merely another program but a systemic approach to congregational learning. It calls for the interdependence of the members and defines the head of the Church (Jesus) clearly by equipping people to depend on his Word. The pastor-equipper encourages bodily growth by teaching people how to feed themselves and by asking questions that help them become more mature. I am so convinced about this that I want to share the several advantages of this pattern of ministry.

☐ *It encourages obedience, not disobedience.* Discovery learning helps people *do* doctrine by focusing on one passage at a time at multiple levels: personal Bible study, group discussions, congregational life and the preached Word. And yet over time, people are exposed to "the whole counsel of God," not just the preacher's pet portions.

☐ *It helps unify the body.* Often pastors fear that small groups will lead to schism or independent fragments within the body. We've found, however, that when all the groups study the same Scripture, we are unified through the Word during the week and the sacra-

ment on Sunday. That's better than being unified through the
personality of the senior pastor!

☐ *It breeds spiritual health.* More people do personal Bible study,
which means Sunday is no longer their spiritual lifeline. Our group
studies often begin with "What did you learn in your personal
study this week?" It encourages accountability.

☐ *It makes the pastor or teaching elder an equipper.* By developing
a congregational curriculum, the Christian worker becomes a theological and biblical resource person rather than a solo entertainer.
It helps give the ministry away without giving it up.[4] Some
thoughts to assist in the process of writing congregational curricula are found in appendix A. This could be used in a day-long
seminar for curriculum writers in your church. Start the day with
an introduction to the biblical book. Then teach how people can
write study questions. And let them work together in clusters during the day on sample passages.

We have been exploring the bold but biblical idea that every member
should learn to study the Bible for himself or herself. This stands in
sharp contrast with the normal situation where people are dependent
on being fed by the same person week by week from the pulpit. But
now we must ask whether one person should do all the preaching.

Equipping Lay Preachers

Pastor John Mutua in Kenya has a problem North Americans should
covet. He cannot train lay preachers quickly enough to keep up with
the growth and multiplication of churches under his care. Every year
I spend three months doing advanced pastoral training with John and
eighteen other church leaders in Kenya. Each pastor or evangelist in
this extension program from Carey Theological College, Vancouver,
must integrate his or her course work in a three-year ministry project.
Our goal is to equip equippers. But the African Brotherhood Church
is growing by twenty-five per cent each year. There are only 108
supported workers for over 800 churches. At last count the church
had 120,000 members. John serves six churches and has been approached by twenty-three believers to form another. For him the
luxury of a seminary-trained, supported pastor for each local church

© 1987 by Rob Portlock. Used by permission.

"They say it's a tough church to preach at."

is unthinkable. He *must* train lay preachers. In contrast we, in North America, think that equipping lay preachers is an optional extra. But there are profound reasons for training lay preachers even where there is a full-time remunerated pastor in each church.

Why Train Lay Preachers?

Biblically we have no option. The ministry of the Word has been the privilege and calling of every believer since the day of Pentecost. I agree with the apostle Peter. If Jesus has ascended and poured out the Spirit then we welcome these "last days" as the fulfillment of Joel 2. We should expect all the sons and daughters of God to prophesy (to speak God's Word with immediacy), young men to see visions and old men to dream dreams (Acts 2:14-18). The precious doctrine of the priesthood of all believers has this practical bearing: Each person functions as a priest when he brings God's Word to another, and the whole believing community is God's priest to the world.

P. T. Forsyth expressed this in his typically pithy way: "The one great preacher in history, I would contend, is the church. And the first

business of the individual preacher is to enable the church to preach.
... He mediates the word to the church from faith to faith, from his
faith to theirs, from one stage of their common faith to another."[5] One
of the qualifications of elders is their being "able to teach" (1 Tim 3:2).
I take this to mean the ability to minister the Word of God in pastoral
situations, whether one to one or with a group. While it is *required*
of elders, it is *possible* for all believers. Martin Luther once said that
when a believer finds himself among non-Christians he needs no
other call or ordination than the fact he is a Christian to preach to
the erring heathen. But when a Christian finds himself among Christians he should not thrust himself forward but rather wait to be called
forth by others to exercise this ministry on behalf of and instead of
others.[6]

We have not only the Bible on our side, but redeemed common
sense. *Strategically,* both the church and the world need to hear from
non-professional Christians. Professional preachers tend to illustrate
their messages from pastor's conferences, religious books and experiences in the daily round of pastoral service without realizing that
they speak from what Abbé Michonneau once called "a clerical culture."[7] The sad truth is that three years of seminary training enculturates a preacher to the church world. Tragically, they often become
incapable of speaking to ordinary people. It is no wonder that while
many church members are impressed with great preachers, the lives
of the ordinary Christians hardly change. In my home church, University Chapel, we have a doctor, a homemaker and a carpenter who
speak two or three times a year. When they rise to bring God's Word
there is an immediate bond between the culture of the speaker and
that of the hearer. They speak with authority and not as a professional
scribe because the truth of their message has not been gleaned from
books but wrung out of their experience. But there is another strategic reason for lay preachers in outreach situations.

The apostle Paul said a shocking thing in 1 Corinthians 9:12 that
is seldom noticed. While he defended the rights of others to earn their
living by the gospel, he denied it for himself for strategic reasons. "We
put up with anything," he said, "rather than *hinder* the gospel of
Christ." Most people think that the gospel will be advanced, not hin-

dered, by multiplying the number of fully supported workers—the more the better. We pity the African pastors like John Mutua who must care for six churches and rely on laypersons to advance the gospel. We wish the African church could have the luxury of one clergy for each church. But perhaps one factor in the spreading Christian movement in Africa is that the work is not hindered by being restricted to fully remunerated pastors. It is essentially a lay movement.

One July Sunday evening, four hundred people came to the Mitaboni church, an African Brotherhood church in a Kenyan village not far from where John Mutua lives. They came to view *Jesus,* a Campus Crusade production that recounts the Gospel of Luke in Swahili. About eighty were saved, and they went out immediately to share their new faith. They won so many more that on Wednesday night, three days later, a throng of eight hundred people (the three-day-old witnessing Christians, the one-day-old Christians and their friends and neighbors) jammed into the Mitaboni church for a second showing. And many more yielded that night to the sovereign and gracious call of Jesus. I maintain that this happens best when undertaken by laypersons, even in North America.

A friend of mine who is a tentmaker, often talks with businesspeople while he travels on planes. More often than not, when they find out he is on his way to speak at a student conference or a church, they will say, "You preachers are just in it for the money." Those of us in supported ministry—as I am—know that most of us are *not* in it for the money. But we had better listen to this criticism and realize that people like this tentmaker will have a special impact on not-yet Christians. It hinders the gospel when we professionalize preaching. The first business of the individual preacher is to enable the church *as a whole* to preach. In the original meaning of the word, it is essentially an amateur activity—those who do it for the love of it with no thought of remuneration.

Further, there is the question of *honesty.* Perhaps a few unique individuals are gifted and anointed by God to bring his prophetic Word to the same congregation twice a Sunday for forty-eight weeks a year. But they are rare. And even these rare pulpit superstars begin to repeat their stories after a few years and eventually must move on to find a new congregation. Why not stay where you are and let God speak through several mouths rather than one? In my opinion even very gifted preachers should not preach more than twice a month to the same people. They need time to apply their sermon to themselves! And God can speak to the preacher through others. Preaching twice a week for life usually creates a credibility gap.

My controversial proposal is that every professional preacher needs to be first of all a listener. Two ears and one mouth is not merely a fact of human anatomy but a requirement for effective preaching. Preachers need to listen twice as much as they speak. They will be pleasantly surprised. God will speak not only to others through lay preachers but to the pastor. The Lord reasoned with Ezekiel about the dilemma of the professional preacher in these disturbing words: "My people come to you, . . . to listen to your words, but they do not put them into practice. . . . Indeed, to them you are nothing more than one who sings love songs with a beautiful voice and plays an instrument well, for they hear your words but do not put them into practice" (Ezek 33:31-32). Equipping lay preachers helps solve this problem, but doing so creates a new set of problems for the pastor. We must explore these now. Equipping pastors must expect problems with the congregation, with would-be preachers and with themselves if they determine to share the preaching ministry.

Anticipating the Problems

The first problem is with the congregation. In a world of rising expectations, the modern pulpiteer is like a gourmet chef trying to find a more enticing way to present the same fare as others. How many ways can you entice people to eat potatoes? In a consumer society, churchgoers are often like restaurant patrons who go where the best food is offered. And many church members are unwilling to exercise patience with a lay preacher who is *growing* in skill. They demand excellence.

But I also want to take the pew-sitter's complaint seriously. The Sunday pulpit ministry must not become the world's greatest amateur hour—in the usual sense of that word. Churches which give everyone a chance at the pulpit are like a gong show without a gong! What I am proposing is the creation of suitable opportunities for people to experiment with a possible preaching ministry, first in a small group, then a devotional address at the annual meeting, then at a youth meeting. Those who give evidence of giftedness and serious intent should eventually be given an opportunity on Sunday. But they must be willing to receive training. Luther did not believe in a professional ministry of the Word, but he did believe in a *trained* ministry.[8] So should we.

Addressing the congregational problem requires foresight and tact. An equipping preacher prepares the congregation weeks ahead for a new voice. When a lay preacher has spoken, a pastor who is secure enough to compliment others will refer in later sermons to some of the unique dimensions of the lay preacher's ministry. He or she will prize the special contribution of the laity. The equipper's task is to bring out into the open the innate gift that lay ministry brings which, if not expounded, would remain on the level of the intuition.

Lay preachers should be introduced *slowly* so the congregation does not feel bludgeoned by change. Ownership of the process is crucial at all levels—elders, board, deacons and congregational meetings. It is folly to move quickly from the same preacher every Sunday to two lay preachers a month. Such tactless equipping will almost certainly guarantee a return to pure professionalism. But a worthy goal is the one embraced by my home church: Teaching-preaching staff persons should do not more than, and generally not less than, sixty per cent of the public ministry. At the time of employing a new staff person these expectations can be carefully negotiated.

A second problem focuses on *the would-be preacher:* The desire to preach may be evil! I have often wondered why there is a line-up three deep to get into the pulpit but no line-up at all for the privilege of washing communion cups. "Ministry" can arise from the dark side of our persons, what Scripture calls "the flesh." Some want public ministry for the *status* it brings, usually if they grew up in a non-affirming environment. Some want it for the *power* they will obtain. Truly, as the proverb says, "The tongue has the power of life and death" (Prov 18:21). Hitler said he threw his words into the crowd as torches and he ignited the people.

Status and power joined by the hunger for *intimacy* form a trinity of wrong reasons to become a preacher. Preaching is a highly personal activity, perhaps especially in the electronic age when the hunger for love and authentic relationships is slaked but not satisfied by the pseudo-intimacy of television. In the biblical Hebraic way of thinking our words express our persons. The whole person comes out of the mouth when he or she speaks. Words are not mere bits of data or wave forms that can be processed or digitalized. Words are persons going out in an active, revealing way. Even more so with God himself whose Word will not return void because of the One who is revealed in the words (Is 55:11).

Without realizing it, those who crave preaching are sometimes subconsciously looking for a vehicle of interpersonal expression. This is normally a good desire, except in someone who is incapable of or unwilling to make intimate relationships outside a high-profile ministry role. With such a person the implied intimacy of the preacher-confessor role creates a pseudo-intimacy in which a person, otherwise inept at making genuine relationships, comes relationally alive. The tragedy is not merely that the public ministry is not congruous with the private, but that the positive reinforcement received for the public ministry may postpone indefinitely the challenge of learning how to make intimate relationships with a person outside of a role.

The problem of the would-be preacher is a complex equipping challenge because we cannot analyze anyone's motives, not even our own. Only God knows the heart. And while the equipping preacher may wisely discern indications of fleshly ambition in those wanting the pulpit he dare not usurp the role of the Holy Spirit. What he must do is wait on the Lord in prayer on behalf of his learning preachers and work hard on preparing them to be preachable persons rather than merely persons who can preach sermons.

So the equipper must wait with reverent and discerning humility. Every sermon begs the question, What kind of person is this that speaks to me? The preacher stands naked in the pulpit. One cannot refrain from revealing oneself any more than one can stop up a hose fully turned on by putting a finger over the outlet. Out of the mouth the heart speaks (Mt 15:18). Eventually the equipping preacher will have an opportunity to help his learning friend cope with the discrepancies of the message and the messenger. For where there is a community of truth and love the very act of ministry is, for both professional and layperson, a furnace of personal transformation and a means of grace to the minister. We must become real or we must get out of the pulpit. John Stott has wisely observed that the preparation of the preacher is more important than the preparation of the sermon.[9]

The problems in the congregation and the would-be preacher are easier to deal with than the problem in the heart of *the equipping preacher*. Giving up personal ministry to release it in others is hard. A few people are psychologically constructed by God to find their highest pleasure in developing the talent of others. They are "born" equippers. But I find that such persons are rarely excellent performers themselves. For the person who loves to preach well and for whom the experience of being anointed in the pulpit is like speaking in tongues—a praise language that uses words to take us beyond words—for such a person the call to equip is a call to self-denial.

Most equipping preachers experience a measure of gift-frustration if they share the pulpit with others. It is best to face this in advance. Even though they believe in their heart it is important to have others preach, they wish they were in the pulpit themselves. But the challenge of making room for others to minister is a call to a deeper spirituality in the equipper. My identity is not to be a preacher but a child of God. What pleases God is not my performance (even as an equipper) but faith active in love. If I "need" to minister I am not letting God minister to my deepest need—my need of him. If I fear that by exalting others I will lose my own "place" in the fellowship, I am being called to find my security not in a role but in my God. Equipping *is* hard, but it is a gracious invitation from our God to go deep. Ironically, by equipping others we equip ourselves in something more vital than ministry skills—being at rest with God, with people and with ourselves. Tragically, many preachers have never gotten to know themselves.

The Prophet's Company
The best way to equip lay preachers is from a prophet's company, such

as existed in Old Testament times around figures like Elijah and
Elisha (1 Kings 19:19-21; 2 Kings 2:7) and in New Testament times
around Jesus and Paul (Acts 17:14-15; 18:1-6; 20:4-6). In the first
three centuries the layperson was active in public preaching and
teaching. The church fathers Justin Martyr and Origen were distinguished members of a "choir of teachers," even though Justin admitted that some of these teachers were often simple-minded *(idiōtai)*
and uneducated. That their ministry was not confined to the church
or to one church is attested by his striking description:

As far as they are able, Christians leave no stone unturned to
spread the faith in all parts of the world. Some, in fact, have done
the work of going round not only to cities but even villages and
country cottages to make others also pious towards God. One could
not say that they did this for the sake of wealth, since sometimes
they do not even accept money for the necessities of life, and if ever
they are compelled to do so by want in this respect, they are content
with what is necessary and no more, even if several people are
willing to share with them and to give them more than they need.[10]

Can one imagine a choir of teachers at, say, First Lutheran Church
in Pincher Creek, composed of a theologically trained pastor, a school-
teacher, a carpenter, a homemaker and a small-business woman—each
sharing in a plural teaching ministry, praying and planning together
the instructional nurture of the church and the church's teaching
mission? Almost universally churches have choirs of singers because
we believe that the ministry of music is too rich to be restricted to
one voice. Why not have a choir of preachers?

In the New Testament, the acts of interpreting Scripture (2 Pet
1:20), being filled with the Spirit (Eph 5:18) and growing to maturity
(Eph 4:13) are *corporate* not individual concepts. The Bible knows
nothing of our granular Western individualism. Becoming a good
preacher is not a solo journey.

In a prophet's company, studying the passage weeks in advance in
connection with an integrated curriculum gives the whole prophet's
company a sense of ownership of the pulpit ministry. Only one
speaks, but he or she does so on behalf of a fellowship. Also, when
preachers in training have studied the passage and sermon in ad-

vance, especially with elders in the choir, they are less likely to abuse the pulpit opportunity.

Such a group can listen to tapes of other gifted preachers and learn skills in oral interpretation. Our culture is highly literate, and merely writing sermons does not result in good oral communication. Almost any group in the world can arrange for a cassette recorder to replay last Sunday's message for learning purposes, and many churches can afford a video recorder to help with gestures, mannerisms and body language.

After two decades of equipping preachers both in the local church and in a theological college, I have concluded that a crucial skill is to learn to say *one* thing well. Jesus did this in his parables. We must do it in the pulpit.

Pastors need such a group of dedicated Bible exegetes, a group that will help *us* find the central thrust of a passage and discern the nerves of the congregation in order to evaluate, plan, pray and study. Pastors rarely get helpful feedback on their own preaching and such a group can give it constructively. The advantages to the would-be-preachers should be obvious.

It is widely known that the post-Christian West has become biblically illiterate. The Reformation put the Bible in the hands of the layperson, but now the layperson has given it back to the biblical scholar and the professional preacher. It is time for a renewed Reformation. The equipping pastor holds the key to this. He or she can engage in a process that results in nurturing the systemic life of the church so that all the people of God hear and do God's words. Our goal is every-member Bible study and a choir of preachers in the church and world. Nothing less than an experiential learning environment will promote this. Michael Eastman comments on the importance of an experiential learning environment:

> Individuals find identity in groups. Warmth, support, spontaneity and mutual care characterize a whole range of unstructured, informal groups and in them the Bible becomes alive, not in a formal, studied way but existentially and life-relatedly. . . . Instead of asking, "How do we help non-readers to read the Bible?" we need to concentrate on another question: "How do people experience en-

counter with the living God in their everyday lives?"[11]
That is the question which must throb in the equipping pastor's brain.
It raises again the crucial role to be played by small groups in the life
of the church, the subject of the next chapter.

Dan Williams, the small group coordinator in my home church,
University Chapel, assumes in the next chapter that you are already
convinced of the crucial place small groups have in releasing lay ministry. For me trying to live the Christian life without a small group
would be like trying to breathe without lungs. If you are not yet
convinced, or are not sure how to proceed with first steps, please
consult one of the excellent books listed in the bibliography for chapter four or read Dan's book, *Seven Myths About Small Groups*
(Downers Grove, Ill.: InterVarsity Press, 1991). Dan takes a diagnos-
tic approach, asking why some groups are not healthy and what good
leadership can bring to that. His approach, consistent with the perspective of this book, is systemic. He thinks that equipping groups
and equipping group leaders must be done together: They are interdependent living elements in systemic group life. And I think he is
right. He writes from a rich experience in churches, parachurch organizations and in consultation settings. So join him on some doctor's
calls to small groups in our church. In this case the doctor is "out"—
visiting the groups and working with the leaders.

Two

Small Group Leaders

By Dan Williams

The patient looks at me and asks, "Do I have a problem?" The patient is large and flabby, listless and unfocused. I suggest that the condition is not terminal but that it does signify a dangerous course. There is an excess of weight and a weak heart. The patient blusters and denies and rationalizes: "But I believe in being open and enjoying life. I need the weight—it comforts me. What if famine sets in? Then I will be protected. And my heart is okay—I just won't exert myself."

The patient I am talking about is a small group in a church or some other organization. The excess weight represents a condition of having too many members, including uncommitted ones; the weak heart, a situation where the group has little or no sense of purpose. The parallel to human disease is quite striking, as is the prognosis: complete health breakdown. Who am I? The group doctor.

The Group Doctor Is In

Being a group doctor is another way of thinking about the job of
coordinating a small group program in a church or parachurch setting. You may be a general practitioner, simply treating groups as part
of a larger ministry; for example, you might be a staff person or
volunteer leader in charge of adult education, with small groups as a
limited part of your task. Or you could be a specialist with small
groups as your main equipping focus. You might practice this special-
ty as a consultant or as part of a permanent staff team in a church
the way I do.

Whatever the situation, every small group equipper faces group
pathologies. You may discover group problems indirectly: gossip from
another church leader about a renegade group, for example. It should
be said here that this often is more a problem of church attitudes than
group attitudes—the so-called renegade group might just be doing the
job that every group is supposed to do: creating an independent identity for itself. In spite of such false alarms you can sometimes find
out about a real issue facing a group through a third party. More
likely, you will find out something more directly, by observing symptoms, such as members not showing up regularly to their group's
meetings, a group only meeting infrequently, a group growing very
large or very small. You might meet discouraged members of a group
in the church lobby or in a committee meeting. Always make it a
policy to ask: "How is your small group going?" That is part of your
job.

Quite often the group facilitator will phone up to have conversation
with you, or a problem will be revealed in "group therapy" (leaders'
meetings) or in the context of a workshop or course. As in human
medicine, the "presenting problem" is sometimes not the root problem.
The group facilitator may say something like: "People aren't showing
up to a group regularly. We seem to have a commitment problem." As
a good group doctor you are thinking: "People's needs aren't being met
and their gifts are not being expressed. They probably have a problem
with not having made a group contract." (I'll explain this later.)

In rare instances group members may invite you in to a meeting
to help them over a hurdle. Don't take the rarity of these invitations

personally: Groups are naturally protective of their life and wary of intrusions, no matter how expert or well-meaning you may be. So you must realize that being invited to group is a great privilege. It is also an encounter that is full of risks. Often the group is in pretty serious shape, otherwise they would not have asked for a "house call." Go, but go carefully. Be open to hearing from the whole patient, that is, every member of the group. Remember that the assessment of the group facilitator about the group can be very different than that shared by other members. In fact, I try to avoid one obvious pitfall by making sure that the whole patient knows that I am coming and what the ground rules are: simply to observe and participate, or to run the meeting, or to make suggestions at the end. Once, as I walked in to a meeting to which I thought the whole group had invited me, one member whom I had never met said, "Here comes the group destroyer." As a group doctor dedicated to the enhancing of life, I have to admit that this hurt! So make sure the whole group has agreed to your visit.

Where Does It Hurt? Seven Group Diseases

The common complaints from ailing house groups can be categorized under seven syndromes. I will provide symptoms, diagnosis and treatment for each. Remember this general rule about treatment: As in human medicine, there has to be some agreement by the "patient" to participate in the healing process.

1. *Extendonitis (The group has outlived itself.)* A basic nurture-fellowship group in the local church concentrates on Bible study, sharing and prayer in a meeting weekly. But consider a group in which the members, relatively few in number, seem to come up with an amazing range of excuses to put off regular meetings. When they do gather, their meetings lack energy, focus and enjoyment. Complaints about the group are different from each person. Comments and questions can become quite personal—"Why haven't you been showing up?" The interchanges may descend into bickering. A malaise of hopeless "stuckness" has settled on the group. When positive suggestions for change do emerge, they generally fall into one of two categories: Let's come up with an ambitious mission project to pull us

together, or let's ask the church for some new members or even a new
leader to shake us up. One final factor to note is that the group has
had two or three good years together before the current state developed.

The last point is the most telling: This group has lasted too long.
Some types of groups, for example, mission groups, accountability
groups, or groups of old friends, can last a lot longer and remain
healthy. But basic nurture-fellowship groups that meet every one or
two weeks exist for a very specific purpose: to develop friendship
between people and create freedom to explore gifts which can then be
used to fulfill visions that develop during the life of the group. Growth
in friendship and freedom and focused vision must happen or such
groups are not doing their job. In light of the purpose of such groups,
consider the following reality statements that will affect your leadership of groups in the church.

☐ True friends do not need a group to sustain their relationship.

☐ True freedom entails releasing people to employ their gifts as
God leads.

☐ The kingdom needs disciples to be dispersed into creative mission.

☐ The visions that develop in a randomly assembled group are
bound to be diverse.

☐ A group program that does not encourage the budding off of
new groups with diverse goals will stagnate.

You may have entered into equipping small groups thinking that
basic nurture-fellowship groups should go on forever. But widespread
experience with small groups shows that groups which have not done
their job in two or three years probably never will. Most basic groups
last one year too long. When they are already in the doldrums they
cry out for help, the cry often coming in the form of a request for new
members or a new mission. The worst thing a group equipper could
do is comply with such a request. Neither new members nor a mission
project can save a group living on borrowed time. Instead, ask to visit
the group, and then gently administer the following medicine from
your "black bag": ask each member to share honestly with the group
what expectation they have of the group and what they would like to

contribute to the group. Another way of doing it is to ask them to describe the ideal group they would like to join if they had a choice. Have someone in the group record the responses.

This is the moment for a seemingly innocent question: How will one group, and in particular this group, satisfy all the expectations mentioned? By this time the light bulb should be going on. The group should be ready for a suggestion that they end in three to six months. This is a moment for genuine affirmation. The group has succeeded in revealing gifts and visions, and now has the delightful responsibility of budding off groups and individuals into new ministry. It is an exciting point in the history of the group, not a depressing one. Naturally their friendships will endure. Personally, I am better friends with some folks now that we are not in a group together!

Try to dissuade them from ending immediately. Ask them to give the group a chance to breathe some fresh air, enjoy some meetings and terminate on a good note. If they need an active goal to make the next months seem worthwhile, then suggest that they contract to pray for clarity in each person's ministry dreams and allow each member to practice their gift in an exaggerated way. For example, if someone is being led to start a new basic nurture-fellowship group, let them take over as group facilitator for a while. Or if someone is keen on pastoring, then let them be in charge of all the group sharing times. People could be motivated (even financed) to take a course or workshop, such as evangelistic Bible study training. In short, the whole period could be full of promise and future possibilities.

On the other hand, the group could resist your conclusions and decide to struggle on against what is perceived as a new enemy: you! If so, they will eventually sputter and die, for it takes common internal purposes, not common external threats, to keep a group healthy. Upon the eventual dissolution of the recalcitrant group, you then have a new job: bandaging up the self-inflicted wounds of the members.

2. *Obesity (The group is too big.)* Another type of unhealthy group presents the following symptoms: When asked how many people belong to the group, a lot of hemming and hahing results. Eventually they will admit that about fifteen or twenty members are "on the list"—but, the group hastens to add, not everyone comes regularly and

there is a "pretty stable core." A little probing by the group doctor will usually reveal a couple of tender spots. Some people at the core of the group are discouraged at the lack of consistent attendance. Further, there exists either a spoken or unspoken contract supporting this dynamic—a contract that actually not everyone supports. This contract of open-ended attendance and/or open-ended membership is often based on a false assumption: that closed groups with temporarily fixed membership and consistent attendance are both unnecessary and unspiritual.

Such an assumption—or others like "Big is beautiful and a sign of success" and "If we grow to twenty we can split into two groups of ten"—frequently leads to groups that are too large. The normal pattern is that a few meetings occur with too many people, and then a gradual decline in attendance sets in as each member's opportunity to be heard and contribute becomes crowded out. Often the problem gets worse as new members are added to shore up the declining meeting size. Facilitators become burned out with administrating too many people. People in the group with a pastoral inclination become overloaded with the burden of caring for so many people, especially those who do not show up very often. Others, longing for the intimacy of a close-knit group of friends, grow tired of welcoming new faces. Mission animators become frustrated because no cohesive group exists to run a project. The group lumbers along and slowly runs out of breath.

A precise diagnosis requires rooting out the controlling assumption behind the obesity and then counteracting with true teaching. If a false spirituality of bigness exists, declare that "small is beautiful." Talk about the advantages of a small membership when it comes to intimacy, study, logistics and so on. If a false spirituality of openness exists, then ask the leading question: "Do you think Jesus would ever have formed a temporarily closed small group for friendship-building and gift development?" They should get the point. Of course, there is nothing wrong with bigness per se; it is just wrong for small groups. And openness can certainly be right for certain mission groups, for example, an evangelistic Bible study where every member has contracted to welcome all comers. It is simply wrong to require every basic group to be so styled.

But how do you get a group to go on a diet? The regimen involves trimming "excess fat" by raising the stakes in the group's contract. The core members who come regularly must decide what they want in a group: If intimacy-building, friendship development and gift discovery are on the list then they can feel free to put a "consistent attendance" clause in the group contract. Communicate this to the fringe members and floating attenders and they usually will drop out and head for "looser" groups. The new streamlined group needs to commit to maintain a healthier size. With human bodies, optimum weight depends on height and build. With groups, membership size depends on the length of the formal meeting. The length must allow time for each member to be significantly involved. An approximate "weight chart" might indicate three members per half hour of meeting; thus, normal church groups meeting for two hours should aim for a maximum of twelve members—though fewer would even be better!

Other surprising things may happen as the group attempts to diet. In the unlikely event that most members want to stay in the renewed group that asks for committed attendance, then be sure to resist the obvious possibility of dividing. Having done the hard work of recommitment, the splitting idea would seem like betrayal of an ideal. Instead, promote the model of breaking down during each meeting into subgroups for activities like sharing, prayer and even study. Worship and mission discussion can happen in the whole group. One important point: Each subgroup should have the same members week to week. This means that the intimacy value of small groups is being approximated, and the likelihood of naturally and gradually spinning off independent groups is increased. Or the whole group may terminate a few months later in the way described above under extendonitis.

Another even rarer possibility is that a majority of the core members may decide to be an explicit mission group which serves a wider group of newcomers to the church or seekers of the faith. In other words, they may decide to be more intentional about their open and large format. In this case, the group must give permission to regulars wanting a close-knit and closed situation to move on to a new group with this character. Interestingly, the remaining mission group, core plus "clients," may even become larger than ever, but this will be the healthy weight of mission muscle rather than the unhealthy weight of fringe fat. Monitoring this type of group requires not a doctor but rather a fitness instructor—someone who can equip and encourage missionaries.

3. *Honeymoonitis (The group is too nice.)* In the early stages of a new group, everyone is trying to make the endeavor work well, just like a couple in a new marriage. So members do not push their expectations too hard or honestly reveal early disappointments. This is why the first contract in a group is often neither comprehensive nor precise. It might say something about Bible study but nothing about worship. Or perhaps the kind of Bible study expected is not identified: in-depth exegesis, personal thoughts about a passage, or silent meditation. Even a simple word like *sharing* needs lots of fine print to define what each person feels about self-disclosure. Furthermore, if sharing is in the contract in any way, it tends to happen at a superficial level in a new group because trust has not yet been built up between members. Certain questions have not been answered which are prerequisites of sharing. Can this group keep confidences? Will it accept me if I am honest? Will I be hit with a lot of unwanted advice?

It is crucial for a new group to make a contract, preferably in writing, concerning the expectations and commitments of the members. Couples preparing for marriage do this today in the process of premarital counseling. It is not a tragedy if a first-time contract needs to be amended a couple of months into a group's life. This happens in a healthy marriage. There is constant negotiation. After a few bad meetings in a group, people may feel more free to state their expectations, for example, that quieter members be given a chance to contribute. The delay in deeper self-disclosure is only natural as people take stock of one another and learn how to study and worship well together.

However, it is entirely different if this status persists, so that months or even years later the doctor finds members still being very careful with one another. For example, the leader asks a question from the Bible study and one person answers. When another question is asked, another person answers. But no one responds to the responders, not even the leader. No one gets excited or disagrees. No one elaborates. Question number three (working their way through the study guide in sequence, as usual) is tossed out, and Fred again launches into a long speech which is not very related to the question. Frieda tries to come in twice, but Fred keeps plowing on. No one stops him. At the end, it is time for the usual sharing. Some safe topics, such as exam finals, a sick aunt or the elders at church are submitted for prayer. Then Frank, who rarely says anything, quietly begins talking about some problems he is having with his boss. People seem uncomfortable. Fred finally offers some authoritative words of advice. The leader then quickly suggests a time of prayer. They pray in order around the circle, with the leader closing. Frieda assigns jobs to some rather reluctant volunteers for the upcoming hospital worship service that she arranges each month. Members are visibly relieved as refreshments are served and superficial bantering begins. Frank leaves first.

How can the equipper help this group? Begin with its contract. How deeply do the members feel comfortable sharing? Could they handle one limited self-disclosure exercise in each meeting? Small group handbooks are full of ideas for building community through creative and progressive sharing. Some study guides, such as Inter-Varsity Press LifeGuides, begin each chapter with a personal question. Ask one member with pastoral gifts to lead this part of the group's life. This person will need to monitor the comfort level of the group at each stage, continually asking if intimacy is outstripping trust. Another suggestion is to find an experienced discussion Bible study leader in your town and ask him or her to lead a model study for the group—the kind where people get so excited that they interrupt one another and in the end everyone leaves with one practical truth they can work on during the week. Another approach is to send a couple of the most promising study leaders to get some training. Then find a group in your town that is hot at worship and prayer. Ask if a couple of members from the pray-in-a-circle-every-night group could drop in a few times to learn that variety and vigor is the spice of small group worship. Finally, run a workshop on consensus decision-making, good group dynamics and group roles. Make sure Fred is there so that he is not surprised when someone interrupts his long speech one day and asks whether he noticed that Frank was trying to say something. And make sure Frieda attends so she can learn about the importance of everyone owning a group project.

A group's members need to learn the hard lesson that only when they begin to share deeply and take risks with one another and only when they discover that they get on one another's nerves can God's grace begin to flow in mutual love and ministry. The alternative is slow death by boredom or neglect. A perpetual honeymoon is terminal.

4. *Schizophrenia (The group has too many identities.)* Some groups have the problem of being in two minds, or ten. Group schizophrenia results from a group's membership having many different expectations. These different goals for the group either remain unspoken or, if spoken, they remain unharmonized. No one attempts to create a compromise. So each member is secretly frustrated, unless they happen to be in charge of a particular meeting—then they let loose with their pet approach. I say secretly frustrated, because this syndrome is limited to a group which is starting out, so the honeymoon tendency prevents honest disclosure of the frustration. The fact that the group is in its early stages is what separates it from extendonitis—identity crisis at the end of a group's life. However, the prescription is similar to that suggested for extendonitis: Spend a meeting sharing expectations and goals for the group. Chances are this was not done well when the group formed. As the expectations become negotiated and formalized into a contract (and, again, I recommend writing the group agreement down), realize that it is not too late to let members who want a different type of contract leave the group. Better a small operation now than major surgery later.

5. *Dwarfism (The group is not growing.)* This one is tricky to diagnose because the symptoms often look like obesity or extendonitis. The group may be very large and people may be joining. The group may have lasted for years. But there are some distinguishing marks of a group that is not growing: The group always meets in the same place, and the host leads the studies and guides most other aspects of the group. With obesity the root cause was a bad assumption about the nature of a spiritual group, and with extendonitis it was an in-

adequate view of the purpose of a spiritual group. In this case the ailment arises from a faulty attitude toward leadership of a spiritual group.

Why do I characterize a group which is large and stable as suffering from dwarfism? Simply because the group is not truly growing. What brings people to the group is a single charismatic leader. This would not be too bad if good group dynamics took over. However, the well-meaning or domineering host allows no one to stretch their muscles in ministry. Most people coming into the group sense the unwritten contract: This is not our group; this is the leader's group. We are just here to receive. The rare initiative of a member is too great a threat to the insecure leader or to the group's status quo. One outcome of the leader's frustration of other members' gifts is voluntary departure or rebellion. Even more tragic, the leader may lull members into a state of dependence and short-circuited growth. An extreme example of this is the excesses of the shepherding movement a few years ago.

Dwarfism is one of the most difficult group conditions to treat. The group leader calls the shots and usually commands great loyalty within the group. Such a leader is often not sympathetic to advice and is wary of other authority. Any intervention by a group doctor may easily be labeled as jealousy or foolish meddling. The best thing you can do is isolate such a group as an anomaly by creating other group options which are more attractive. Watch for drop-outs and orient them to a different type of group experience. At the same time, remain on good terms with the one-person-show leader. Avoid telling them to do less. Instead, try to give them a vision for an even bigger ministry: letting some of their members move into leadership of new groups (after you retrain them). Show them how birthing many independent groups would even be more exciting and strategic than shepherding one flock. If possible, do not make strong-minded leaders into martyrs. They often have great gifts to offer the church. It is only in rare and extreme cases that an isolated flock becomes cancerous and needs heavy radiation from church authorities. The fall-out is usually as bad as the disease.

6. *Archiphobia (The group is afraid of leadership.)* I confess I made

up this word from *arch-*, the Greek word which means chief or superior. This is a modern phenomenon which afflicts small group work no less than other structures in society. Anxiety about totalitarianism, as described under dwarfism above, leads to democracy gone wild when everyone is in charge, and anarchy results.

The observant reader might have noticed that my treatment for honeymoonitis made suggestions for every type of leadership role in the group apart from the designated leader. This was deliberate. I wanted to stress the need to draw out and enhance everyone's leadership contribution in order to create a more satisfying group experience. It is quite right to resist the notion that all progress depends on a single leader. However, it is quite wrong to deny the importance of a facilitator or coordinator for every small group. As long as the group carefully defines that role in terms of serving and equipping, there is no need for a phobic response.

Two debilitating patterns emerge in the absence of a designated leader. First, the group is imbalanced. Through the Spirit, good things happen even in a group missing a helmsman. But the lack of a helmsman produces what could be described as a hormonal imbalance. People with a damaged endocrine gland, for example, the thyroid, act in an erratic manner. Likewise, groups without oversight flounder to some extent. Contracts are non-existent or not renewed. Evaluation is spotty. No one asks hard questions about the group's life, so it enters a rut. Bible study becomes routine. Worship is stale. Sharing stays at the same level. Mission threatens to take over or to disappear, sometimes in cycles akin to manic-depression. Good facilitators or coordinators help to balance the components of group life and create an environment of steady development where people feel free to share their gifts.

The second bad pattern that surfaces in the "leaderless group" is the secret leader. Some sociologists maintain that the leader role will always be filled in a group. The problem is that unacknowledged, clandestine leaders have no social controls on them. They can work manipulatively and without accountability. One of the great ironies of group work and international politics is that communistic systems easily transform into dictatorial systems. In short, archiphobia can lead to dwarfism. This is literally illustrated by the group of fugitives, in fact dwarf thieves, in the movie *Time Bandits,* where the following conversation takes place:

"Do you want to be leader of this gang?"

"No, we agreed, no leader."

"Right. So shut up and do as I say."

What is the group doctor to do? Suggest appointing a facilitator. Or, if this is too threatening, try two or three co-leaders. One approach is simply to provide a clear job description and ask the group to recognize who fits the bill. Often the person who does the phoning and prints up schedules is the one you are looking for. Then provide follow-up training to fine-tune the servant skills of the new leader. If the group is still nervous, have them take on a coordinator for a short trial period and then evaluate. All they have to lose is confusion.

7. *Autism (The group is absorbed in itself.)* It seems fitting that autism is mostly an affliction of children because maturing into true adulthood is almost by definition the opposite of autism. Rather than morbid absorption in fantasy at the expense of a proper response to the environment, an adult has healthy relationships with the outside world. This may be equally said of small groups: The maturing process of a group requires an active acknowledgment that life exists beyond its borders. In other words, mission must be part of every healthy small group. This must be true—even if only embryonically—from the very first meeting. A brand-new group must at least be committed to support each member's personal witness outside the group. Most basic groups will go further before they end and manage a one-time mission project, for example, an evangelistic dinner party. Some may even participate in a regular mission expression.

The important thing is that later mission developments, and maturing in general, depend on early commitments to an outward focus. Otherwise, self-absorption sets in amazingly fast. It is a normal process for growing friends to become close and then closed off. It is a good and inevitable result to grow close, but kingdom friends must resist the latter trend to closedness. Resisting self-preoccupation does not require that groups have open membership. It merely means including a mission mentality in your first and all subsequent contracts, combined with an understanding that you are not forming an eternal group and therefore plan to disperse into new mission expressions upon termination.

In the world of groups, both schizophrenia and archiphobia can lead to autism. Bad contracting does not produce good mission. Good contracts require honest group disclosure and compromise, which in turn require able leadership. So autism has its roots in the beginning of a group. However, it is also true that the condition can creep in with the onset of extendonitis. There is no harder shell to crack than that surrounding a tired, inbred group that has been going too long.

The intervention for autism depends on the stage of the group. In a young group, find a leader among the membership to help the group re-contract with a mission dimension included. In a mature group suffering extendonitis (with accompanying autism), see the guidelines given for the first syndrome above.

The Best Medicine Is Prevention

Having offered a limited textbook of group pathology, I want to offer one clear implication: As with human wellness, the best cure is to avoid getting sick in the first place. After all, only one usage of the Greek word *katartismos* (equipping) relates to medicine—"setting of a bone." The other nuances are "preparation" and "creation." These words suggest what could be called preventative medicine. I have admitted more than once that the treatments for sick groups are hardly foolproof, even assuming that a group is open to your doctoring. So preventions are clearly preferred over interventions. Preventative medicine needs to be practiced in three major areas.

☐ *Teach healthy patterns to whole groups not just facilitators.* The best time to do this is when newcomers are being oriented to your church or organization, or when new groups are being established. This is a systemic approach to group formation in harmony with the theme of this book.

☐ *Teach small group facilitators the limits of their job description not just the skills required to fulfill their task.* The best way to do this is to ensure that group members know almost as much as the leader when it comes to how a good group operates. Once again, equip the group not just the leader.

☐ *Work with the whole church system to foster healthy groups.* Environmental engineering is required so that the unhealthy life of a fellowship does not become codependent with unhealthy small groups in that fellowship. For example, the church-wide dwarfism which results from one-person shows in a pulpit ministry in turn enables bad group leadership models to persist. Where lay leadership has not been generally released in a church, small groups will be weak. If the staff or elders impose a top-down style of management, trying to get every group to follow the same pattern, then identity crises will result. In this case, the cause will not be internal schizophrenia but rather the quenching of the Spirit by regulations imposed on the groups from outside. The simple truth is this: Healthy small groups and a healthy church environment are interrelated. To equip good groups we must equip the church as a whole. The equipping pastor has an awesome opportunity to do this.

Ultimately, I would like to see group doctors put out of business by host churches that facilitate good group births and healthy group development. In reality, the equipping pastor is always working simultaneously with health and sickness. So until the disease-free day arrives, the following check-up inventory will prove a useful way of measuring how healthy each group is in your church.

DOCTOR'S CHECK-UP:
THE QUALITY OF SMALL GROUP LIFE

Directions: Circle closest description of your small group. Add up the results (maximum total is 50). A group measuring above 35 is doing well. A group between 35 and 20 needs some attention. A group measuring below 20 needs intensive care.

Leadership
1. A domineering leader in charge
2. "No leader" mentality
3. Designated leader or group coordinator recognized
4. Other leadership gifts being recognized and employed
5. New small groups and coordinators being spawned

Contract
1. Haven't thought about it
2. Considered it informally
3. Considered formally and regularly with lots of discussion
4. Written down and submitted to the church
5. (In a group over two years old) a clause to end in six months included

Development
1. No sense of progress from phase to phase for over 2 years
2. Have some sense of review and evaluation occasionally
3. A formal review and re-contracting at specified intervals
4. Concerted desire to deepen group life with each new cycle
5. A plan to have the group end after 2 or 3 years

Membership
1. Completely open membership—anyone can show up at any time, or over 12 members
2. Modified open—additions can be negotiated any time
3. Completely closed—no new members for over 2 years
4. Modified closed—additions only during re-contracting
5. Open membership as part of mission group contract

Nurture
1. Never study the Bible
2. A Bible lecture as the staple diet
3. Discovery Bible discussion as staple, plus variation
4. Gifted discussion leaders recognized and regularly used
5. Using curriculum with personal study and linked to sermon

Community
1. The group is very polite and stiff
2. The leader models vulnerability, openness to conflict
3. Questions are asked which broaden and deepen sharing
4. There is sensitivity to stages and roles of group life
5. Pastors are recognized; the group is relaxed & humorous

Worship
1. Worship is not discussed or is only defined by singing
2. Aggressive people impose a worship agenda on weak members
3. Worship is contracted, taught on, evaluated
4. There is a freedom to move beyond just songs and prayer
5. Freedom to experiment; some whole meetings of worship

Mission
1. A sense of mission is not set in the first meeting
2. There is a concerted ministry to needy members
3. Personal witness is regularly encouraged and prayed for

4. A mission project is contracted
5. The group is about to bud off a mission group

Planning
1. Meetings and other activities are planned a week ahead
2. There are a balance of components and a varied schedule
3. Planning happens 2-3 months ahead, with a journal kept
4. A team of leaders plan each meeting in some detail
5. Regular feedback is given to leaders by the group

Congregation
1. The group acts completely independently
2. The group follows the directions of the church hierarchy
3. The group has a measure of autonomy and authority
4. Coordinator attends leader meetings
5. Coordinator & group are pastorally related to an elder

Three

Lay Pastors & Caregivers

*There are few, if any, ways that
ministers can invest their professional
expertise that pay richer dividends
than helping to equip lay careers.*[1]
Howard Clinebell

Last week I felt like tearing the phone off the wall!" As I said
this I leaned over to my pastor-friend, Ben Smith, who had graciously
asked how things were going. That is what you are supposed to ask
at a pastors' prayer group.

He replied with empathy, "I have often felt like that myself—until
yesterday. I was near the phone, and a young man called who desper-
ately needed help. He was a homosexual who had lost his job teaching
in northern Alberta and was on his way home to start again. I think
he was really open to spiritual realities."

"Yes," I said, "and his name was Norman; he is twenty-three years
old, has a church background and was once preparing for the ministry. He has a sister in Charlottetown, Prince Edward Island, and you
probably bought him a train ticket at your own expense to get home,
right?"

Ben dropped his jaw with disbelief and asked, "How did you know?"

"Because," I said, "I put him on the train the day before!"

And so it goes. Sometimes just dealing with the charlatans outside, let alone the true sheep on the inside of the fold, is enough to make one want to quit pastoral ministry.

In my first pastorate, in the inner city of Montreal, I was a frustrated pastor. After keeping up the mailing list and getting the bulletin out on time, I spent much of my time caring for the sheep who were lying on their backs kicking. In those days a deacon, Bill Maxwell, was my spiritual friend, and he took me out for coffee every morning to care for me. One day, when I confided that I was going to resign, he asked why. I sighed, "I feel like a firefighter. I hear about some growing fire of discontent and go there to put it out only to hear of another one somewhere else. I'm tired of putting out fires."

This dear brother replied, "But you're the best damn firefighter we ever had!" It was a delightful backhanded compliment. And it gave me the courage to go on exploring how, instead of doing all the pastoral ministry, I might equip some of the saints to do pastoral ministry. That is the subject of this chapter. But before we explore the systemic, body approach to equipping lay pastors I must ask an important question.

Whatever Happened to the Lay Pastor?

I mentioned that the word *laity* does not mean in the Bible what it has come to mean in modern speech. The laity *(laos)* are those who have the supreme dignity of being God's people (1 Pet 2:9-10). What God did through the clergy in the Old Testament—prophets, priests and kings—he now does through all the people. The usual Greek word for layperson *(laikos)* in the sense of "belonging to the common people, as distinct from clergy, is *never* used in the New Testament and is not used to describe a Christian until Clement of Rome in A. D. 95. The inspired authors of the New Testament took the usual word for a crowd *(laos)* and invested in this word all that the people of God had come to be under the Old Covenant. It does not mean uneducated or incompetent even though Peter and John were called laypersons *(idiōtēs)* in this sense by the Jewish professional religionists who marveled at their bold preaching (Acts 4:13). Even the Greek word for clergy *(klēros)* is never used in the New Testament for a special class of ministers; rather, it denotes the privilege and share that all Christians inherit when they are included by Christ in God's family (Col 1:12). So, surprisingly the church is without laypersons (in the usual sense), while every member is a clergyperson!

Another word for the church, *ekklēsia,* from which we get the English word *ecclesiastical,* means a gathered people. The English word *congregation* communicates part of the meaning of *ekklēsia.* This too guarantees the universality of ministry in the congregation because the "call" that constitutes the "gathered" or "called-together" people comes to all the saints (Eph 4:1). Pastoral care is a "one-another" responsibility in the New Testament, part of the calling of the congregation.

Household (Gal 6:10; Eph 2:19) is another word for church in the New Testament, and this is especially meaningful in the earliest years when many churches met in homes (Rom 16:11; 2 Tim 4:19). The church is a family-style community in which relationships are covenantal rather than institutional and contractual. It is salutary to reflect what happened when churches moved from homes to converted pagan temples or specially built buildings because the process of doing this involved moving the altar from the home to the church. As we have already discovered, some family-style ministry can be recovered in house groups.

The Empowering Vision of the New Testament Church

In the earliest church described and prescribed on the pages of the New Testament, pastoral care was mainly the responsibility of the people. When Paul had severe problems in Corinth—incest being just one—he did not write to the elders to get their act together. Rather, he wrote both letters to the church. It is the church that is responsible for discipline and pastoral care. Therefore Paul's letters are filled with motivating injunctions to care for one another (Eph 4:25-32 is an example). Every major renewal has been fired by the vision of the New Testament Church. Central to that vision is the whole people *(laos)* of God enlivened by the Spirit to live to the praise of God's glory in the world. This is true of the Baptist movement, the English Methodist movement and the Plymouth Brethren. Before the Protestant Reformation, various renewal movements recovered the lay principle. During the Middle Ages, a worldly church and a longing for evangelical simplicity sparked the laity to do something about it; the Cathars, the Waldensians, the Lollards were essentially lay movements of persons hungry for authentic Christianity. People like Peter Waldes, Dante and Francis of Assisi are a refreshing alternative lay image to the submissive, docile layperson so often encountered in the Middle Ages.[2] The Reformation, in its driving power, both on the continent and England, was mainly a lay movement, though unfortunately the magisterial Reformers did not provide an adequate ecclesiology for their theology of the priesthood (and pastorhood) of all believers.

The public influences of church history were frequently laypersons. The great Reformer John Calvin is one of the most conspicuous examples in Christian history of a layperson who became a self-made theologian. His famous *Institutes* was not the work of a clergyman or a theologian but a layperson. In the seventeenth century, lay theologians like Bunyan, Milton, Leibniz and Hugo Grotius were formative. Another layman, Nikolaus von Zinzendorf, influenced by the Moravian Brethren, molded a little group of lay men and women for world mission.[3] Sir Thomas More and William Wilberforce were two laypersons who expressed their Christian vocation in the political domain.

In our own century the layman John R. Mott was influential in sparking student missions. Another layman, Englishman Howard Guinness, sold his sports equipment to buy passage to Canada in order to bring InterVarsity Christian Fellowship (as it came to be called) to Canada. Renewal movements in our own day—the small group movement, charismatic renewal and the signs and wonders movement—have all looked to the New Testament church for an empowering vision.

The Layman in Christian History, edited by Stephen Neill, is a superb attempt to rewrite church history in terms of the layperson's life and mission. Here are some discoveries about the ancient church of A.D. 30-313.

☐ *The layperson fully participated in the celebration of the sacraments.* Referring to the layman's ordination to the royal priesthood by baptism, Irenaeus of Gaul said, "All who are justified though Christ have the sacerdotal order."[4] At the believer's baptism anointing oil was applied, just as Israel's kings and priests had been consecrated. Of this Tertullian argued that baptismal ordination qualified the recipient to baptize others, at least occasionally:

> Thereupon as we come forth from the laver, we are anointed with the holy unction, just as in the Old Dispensation priests were anointed with the oil from the horn of the altar. Whence the term *Christus,* from the chrism which is the anointing, a name that is now appropriated to the Lord.[5]

(One has to imagine Deacon Brown in Pumpkin Center Baptist Church conducting a baptism while the pastor sits with his family.)

☐ *The layperson conducted worship.* Admittedly, in the Greco-Roman world it was ordinarily among "heretics" that in the absence of clergy laypersons would conduct the eucharist. It was after Tertullian became a Montanist (the member of a radical renewal sect) that he said, "For where three are, there is the Church, albeit they be laics."[6] Tertullian describes an agape love-feast that would delight the heart of any house group today: "After washing of hands and the lighting of lamps individual members are invited to stand out and sing to the best of their ability either from sacred scriptures or something of their own composing."[7] (This sounds delightfully near a renewal praise service in First Presbyterian Church!)

☐ *The layperson was active in church discipline and confession.* Eusebius describes how a rural bishop repented and returned to the orthodox community, asking for forgiveness "rolling at the feet not only of those in the clergy but also of the laics."[8] Primarily it was a layperson who received confessions and forgave in the name of Jesus, fulfilling the exhortation of James 5:16. (Can one imagine today, in the Evangelical Free Church of Spuzzum, a repentant adulterer turning for healing and forgiveness not to the pastor but to his house-group leader, a layperson?)

☐ *Laypersons cast out demons and renounced Satan's works.* Justin Martyr comments on how Christian exorcists were successful in doing what frustrated others: "When all other exorcists and sayers of charms and sellers of drugs failed, they (lay prayer healers) have healed them, and still do heal, sapping the power of the demons who hold them, and driving them out."[9] Origen notes that "it is mostly people quite untrained who do this work . . . by such means as the simpler kind of man might be able to use."[10] (One must imagine that the most experienced and discerning in spiritual warfare at St. John's Community Church were laypersons.)

The Demise of the Lay Pastor

What happened? Truly, the priesthood of all believers can be lost in a single generation. It is hard for us even to imagine a church in which a congregational meeting elects a bishop, in which any member in good standing may baptize another, in which women can lay hands of commissioning to the lay ministry on a woman who was just baptized, in which laypersons preside at great theological debates and regularly preach in pulpit and town hall. We can only make ourselves available to a sustained renewal of lay ministry if we understand what did happen to lay ministry and mission.

Some lay pastors were clericized, separated by office, title and role from other lay ministers. This process is well documented.[11] It is a sad thing indeed to read how the laity were reduced to congregational singing as early as the fourth century[12] and people were arranged in the church in a hierarchical order. The sources of this were threefold: First, the secular leadership model of the magistrate *(klēros)* and the uneducated laity; second, the carry-over from the Old Testament of a formalized separated priesthood; third, the popular elevation of the sacraments as holy mysteries requiring a holy person as their administrators.[13]

Other lay pastors were eclipsed by the clergy. By the fourth century, even the mundane work of administering finances and church property became the preserve of the clergy.[14] Some shreds of lay participation in ministry as full partners with the clergy remained, but this was chiefly among groups like the Donatists, which were regarded as heretical. Today we might think of them as renewal movements!

One glorious exception to the trend is the election of Ambrose to be bishop by the laity. "In November 274 ... Ambrose was acclaimed bishop by the thronging crowd in the cathedral of Milan, and though he was a layman at the time, this example of *vox populi, vox Dei* [the voice of the people as the voice of God] was adjudged binding."[15]

For the most part, however, the church absorbed secular models of leadership from the trade and dramatic guilds, financial and burial societies, that abounded in the Greek world. These associations operated in a hierarchical leadership model, and it was all too easy for the church to promote one of the elders to become a bishop-president.[16]

Lay pastors were trivialized. Noting how even to the educated fifth-century Christian laymen enriched the church with theological reflection and forced the clergy to come to terms with their arguments, William Frend asks: "Why did this movement [lay theological movement] fail to last? Why had Europe to wait for a thousand years before the lay theologian reappeared?"[17] Frend offers some possibilities: Culture died; the future became unthinkable; an other-worldly association developed. In sum, the life and mission of the ordinary Christian was trivialized in comparison with the monk or the ordained clergyperson.

Even the Protestant Reformation did not unpack the implications of being a fully equipped church: all believers priests in an empowered, gifted community. The gospel of justification by faith came to the fore again, but the priesthood of this gospel was viewed in the light of one's individual relationship to God rather than a corporate responsibility to minister to one another and the world. The one-bishop rule that emerged in the second and third centuries, partly to cope with pressures on doctrine and discipline within the church,[18] was virtually unchallenged. It is still with us today.

In short laypersons were lost *in the world* through secularism and eclipsed *in the church* by the clergy. The same forces work in every generation. So the challenge of pastoring the members of a church boils down to a very simple choice: You can do it yourself, or you get the church to pastor the people. Neither choice is easy, but the latter leads to the rich rewards of equipping the saints for the work of the ministry (Eph 4:11-12).

Having seen that the present one-person-pastor model is not uni-

versally supported by Scripture or history, we must now address the
problem that the present pattern simply does not work.

Whatever Happened to the Omnicompetent Pastor?

Since 1963 when Bill challenged me to put my convictions into practice, there has been a change of ethos in the professional ministry. In
those days when one was ordained, a well-meaning denominational
official would lay an intolerable burden on the young pastor's
shoulders: preacher, worship leader, counselor, pastor, evangelist, administrator, healer. One would think, to hear such ministerial charges,
that the whole charismatic ministry of the church could be invested
in one person. But it cannot. The pastor cannot do it alone and knows
this deep inside. And the people make an implicit agreement with the
pastor that while he or she cannot do all the ministry, they will expect
him or her to try and do it well. In this chapter we are exploring the
release of laity into merely *one* facet of the traditional pastor's role:
pastoral care. But how complex and varied even this one facet is. Here
is a list of pastoral ministries taking place even in a small church:
visitation, pastoral counseling, prayer counseling, marriage ministries,
family ministry, spiritual friendship and direction, healing and ministering to the sick, mediation and reconciliation, discipline, and caring
for people in the rites of passage. (A more detailed list can be found
at the end of this chapter.) Even this impressive list does not quite
cover the waterfront. We could have included pastoring through
preaching and through structured small groups, two matters we have
already explored. We also have not mentioned the liturgical, sacramental and formal pastoral ministries, including administering the
sacraments of eucharist and baptism, ministries on which there is
considerable difference of opinion of whether the unordained should
officiate. Let's leave the controversial ones aside and concentrate on
the ten named above.

The Moses Principle: Delegation

Most books on lay pastoral care today operate on the Moses principle.
His father-in-law, Jethro, found Moses wearing himself out meeting
everyone's needs and confronted him. "What you are doing is not good"

(Ex 18:17). What follows is a biblical case study in good management. Jethro got Moses to delegate most of his work to "capable men" (18:21) who supervised groups of thousands, hundreds, fifties and tens. "Have them serve as judges for the people at all times," Jethro advised, "but have them bring every difficult case to you; the simple cases they can decide themselves. This will make your load lighter, because they will share it with you" (18:22). Here then is one answer for the omnicompetent pastor: delegation. It is certainly better than being worn out by pastoral ministry. But is it good enough? Essentially it leaves the pastor in charge of his own ministry and responsible for recruitment, training and selection of the volunteers to help him. Only cases too hard for the subordinate get bumped to the superior.

The Moses principle is a great step forward. For many overworked pastors today, it could be a quantum leap. But as a pattern for pastoral ministry under the New Covenant, it is something less than adequate. Under the New Covenant the whole church is a gifted people (1 Cor 12), a priestly people (1 Pet 2:9-10), an empowered people (Eph 1:19-20) and a servant people (Jn 13:14). Now that Christ has made us *all* competent to be ministers of a new covenant (2 Cor 3:7-18), the pastor's job is not to lighten his own pastoral care load by expeditious delegation to willing and trained volunteers. Rather, according to Ephesians 4:11-12, the pastor-teacher is called to equip the saints *to do their own ministry,* not the pastor's. So what we are exploring in this chapter is not getting the pastor's job done by lay assistants, but rather *getting the whole church to pastor the saints.* One facet of this principle is the importance of pastors relinquishing lay pastoral ministries for which they are neither called nor equipped.

Let me take prayer counseling, or inner healing as it is sometimes called, as an example. It is not *my* ministry as a pastor, but it appears to be a ministry that God wants me to equip in the local church where I serve. In pastoral experience, I discovered that merely preaching and counseling forgiveness does not always bring release from the deep memories of people's lives—of being unwanted (or perhaps given in adoption or nearly aborted), or of being sexually or physically abused or of suffering a profound trauma as a child. Recurring nightmares, the inability to enjoy the sex act as a married adult, or an inappropriately triggered volcanic anger are symptoms, among others, which often indicate a need for healing of memories, or soul-healing as it is sometimes called.

My wife stumbled on this ministry accidentally at a conference where, by mistake, she was assumed to be one of the leaders and was drawn into a leadership group praying for the profound healing of a person's past. What Gail experienced convinced her that God could do something more than she had witnessed him do through her counseling ministry. In company with another experienced prayer counselor, she began praying for individuals to experience inner healing. But this was not *my* ministry as a pastor. In fact, I was skeptical and cautious, so much so that I followed her to a conference by Rita Bennett[19] at which I had intended to "snoopervise." But the conference was designed for participation, not passive observation. I found myself dealing with a major hurt during my teen years, the feeling of non-affirmation by my parents that has been a major factor in my predisposition to public ministry situations where I gain status and approval. Subsequent to this conference, I have prayed for others in this way, sometimes as my wife's assistant. But in no way have I "delegated" that ministry. It was not mine to delegate. Nor am I the one to which referral should be made in very difficult cases—Gail and her ministry partners know more about this ministry than I do. My task as an equipping pastor is to make room for what God is doing through members of the church in this ministry, to stand ready to assist in the development of this ministry.

So the Moses principle is not enough. The equipping pastor will not be satisfied until all the laity of God take up pastoral ministry in mutual care in the many ways God calls and gives gifts in the local church. But modern pastors are not merely frustrated in their attempt to follow biblical models. They are impacted by powerful social forces in the modern world. One is the search for excellence in everything, including pastoral care. This has led to a specialization mania even in ministry.

The Professional Principle: Specialized Pastoral Care
Specialization has changed both the expectations of pastor and people.

In an age when people insist on being referred to cardiac specialists for a heart-murmur complaint, when the general physician, incorrectly in my opinion, is frequently seen as a mere referral center, the omnicompetent pastor is as antiquated as the witch doctor in a modern African city. Few pastors today feel capable of being an excellent preacher and, at the same time, competent in counseling someone struggling with homosexuality. So wherever possible, we hire a team, and one of those team members is usually designated as the minister of pastoral care. That person quickly realizes, however, that the job is still too big for one person to do even as a pastoral care specialist. We must have sub-specialty professionals, or so we think.

The professional has a quasi-unique function for which he or she has been carefully trained. Amateurs are discouraged from entering this field, on the assumption that the professional can do it better. The person must necessarily be supported and employed doing this, because it is impossible to gain an appropriate level of expertise by doing it part-time. Life is too short, and the information is too overwhelming for a person to keep up in more than one field. These highly specialized functions performed by a professional are seen as roughly interchangeable, so that the technical procedure could be performed by another with the same skills. One such professional skill is pastoral care. The general care of the people for which older pastors were distinguished as true lovers of the flock, has been largely replaced by professionalized specialists. Who, after all, feels competent to deal with sexual abuse or substance addiction, except a professionally trained counselor?

With the exception of "pastoral counseling," which cannot be exactly equated with the entire "cure of souls" ministry which once belonged to the church, counseling has largely passed out of the church into the hands of secular or Christian professionals. But in the case of counseling, an amateur might be the best person.

The word *amateur* in its original meaning refers to one who does something for the love of it. People have a deep need to be loved and to love, not because it is someone's job, but because it is in someone's heart. Everyone needs a friend, and calling a psychiatrist or a licensed counselor a "professional friend" is a misnomer. Love can never be professionalized. It cannot be sold or hired. So by restricting counseling to those with the educational requirements, degrees and state or provincial qualifications, we have stolen a crucial ministry from the people of God, not merely the pastor. The pastor, now intimidated by the burgeoning expertise of the counseling profession, refers his or her hardest cases to the secular specialist. The Joint Commission on Mental Illness and Health (USA) found through a national survey that about half the people seeking counseling went to a clergyman first and were either referred to a mental health specialist or else ignored.[20] Keith Gaetz, a counselor who is also one of my students at Regent College, concludes, "The church is apparently one of the greatest referral agencies to what has become a multi-billion dollar a year industry."[21]

We cannot find the solution to the pastoral care dilemma in either routine referral to health care officers *or* in hiring a professional counselor on the church staff team. What we need is a ministry of the whole body, the multi-faceted gifting of God in the local church to care for the people in the church. It will take the whole church to minister to the whole church. The ministry of the people of God must necessarily be amateur. Those who do it for love (whether in Christian service careers or dedicated volunteers)—are the only ones worth consulting for pastoral help. Our deepest need is to love and be loved. A loveless specialized pastor would leave the soul restless and weary. The professionalism of Western society has become so idolatrous that one can only pursue technique safely when one has determined in one's heart that love is the only essential. Like alcohol, technique or technology in ministry is a dangerous addictive that must be controlled. So in the kingdom of God the most important jobs must be given to amateurs, the least consequential to professionals. It is the world that is topsy-turvy, not the kingdom.

Letting the Church Pastor the Church!
Once again it appears that lay pastoral care is an idea whose time has come. A chorus of voices maintain that nonprofessional caregivers can, with the right training and supervision, be more effective in many cases than professionals. Robert R. Carkhuff, a pioneer in the

field of training lay helpers, comments on the research literature, "Briefly, the available evidence indicates that lay training programs have been more effective [than professionalized care] in demonstrating change on indexes that measure constructive helpee change."[22] Self-help groups like Alcoholics Anonymous have long known the power of peer therapy for people with clear recognition of a profound need, but now a wide variety of care and counseling works are being done by paraprofessionals with great success. The church is catching on to this, and a few good books have been written, among them Howard Stone's *The Caring Church* and Melvin J. Steinbron's *Can the Pastor Do It Alone?* Years ago Kenneth Haugk, a pastor and clinical psychologist in St. Louis, responded to the low level of ownership of pastoral care in his church by starting a training program for lay caregiving known as The Stephen Ministries.[23]

Besides training the pastor to train lay caregivers, this superb organization remains available for help and continuing supervision of the caregivers, a critical factor in the ongoing success of any lay pastoral program. But it will take more than a program to release lay pastors in the local church. The problem is not programmatic but systemic. It relates to the fundamental relational, theological, structural and spiritual life of the local church. As we will see throughout this book, releasing lay ministry involves *equipping the church to equip the saints*. In other words, pastoral care is a matter of the total life of the church, the quality of its relational life and spirituality. When the church is healthy, the people pastor one another (Col 3:12-17; Eph 4:15—5:2). To make a beginning we will now explore some practical steps in equipping lay pastors and caregivers.

Start with the Heart

My assumption is that Jesus, not the pastor, is the head of the church. No human ecclesiastical leader is ever called the head of the church in the New Testament. Christ, as head, will provide the gifts and people for all the pastoral ministries he wants accomplished. He is the ultimate equipper. He gives gifts (Eph 4:11-12) and through the Spirit empowers people for works of service (Acts 1:8). He orchestrates the gift-mix of the local congregation as he sees fit (1 Cor 12:11). He supplies the connections or "joints" (Eph 4:16) in the body so that growth into his humanity will take place through the interdependence of the members. Usually Jesus makes us *want* to do his will. His purpose for us is written into the fibers of our personality and the regenerated motivation which comes through conversion. So the first thing we need to do is not to train lay pastors but to discover them!

A questionnaire based on the ten pastoral care ministries listed at the beginning of the chapter can be used to invite people to indicate if they are strongly or weakly motivated to perform each of these ministries. (You will find a sample questionnaire at the end of this chapter.) Another approach, again with proper preparation through preaching and explanation, is to give out 3 x 5 cards in a Sunday service and ask people to indicate what they would really like to do for God if time, talent and training (the three easiest things to do something about) were not obstacles. The response will be amazing. Many people will indicate a heart interest in pastoring. The equipping pastor is looking for the pastoral heart among the people of God.

Pastors are interested in people of all sorts and conditions. They are concerned with a person's eternal destiny and the need to deepen the conversion experience. They do not want people to depend on them in a sick way, but to learn to be dependent on God. Pastors are determined to make no distinctions between people in estimating their ultimate value. They are determined never to give anyone up for lost. They breathe the aroma of God's presence and help people to know that God loves them. As one person said, "I need God's love with skin on." They usually can be identified simply because they already have "a flock," a group of people who relate consistently to them, often clustered around them when a Sunday service is over. A pastor and a sensitive group of lay leaders or elders can often identify the real pastors of the church even if they do not volunteer themselves when you announce a lay pastor's training group.

Develop an Equipping Group

Lay pastors need an environment to grow in ministry, and there is hardly a better one than a small group. For the senior pastor, investment in this group can be one of the most rewarding dimensions of local church leadership, not merely because it provides an opportunity for delegating some of his or her own ministry, but because the pastor will receive ministry from those he or she is equipping. As Samuel Southard says in *Comprehensive Pastoral Care,* "The priorities of a pastor's services are reversed in this system. Instead of going first to the sick and lonely, the pastor will spend most of the time and attention with the healthy members who then become ministers to the sick and lonely."[24]

The Stephen Ministry program has been widely used as a training resource for such a group of lay pastors. Melvin J. Steinbron, author of *Can the Pastor Do It Alone?,* proposes advertising and inviting people to a twelve-unit fifteen-hour seminar over a Saturday and Sunday. His units include the following themes:

1. The Concept of Lay People Pastoring
2. The Biblical Basis
3. Who Needs It?
4. What a Lay Pastor Does
5. Pastoral Supervision
6. Being Professional
7. Being Precedes Doing
8. Imperatives for Personal Spiritual Health
9. The Anatomy of a Visit
10. Authority to Pastor
11. The Lay Pastor Listens
12. Confidentiality

Commissioning them, Steinbron sends out the trained lay pastors on their first visit, usually in the company of a more experienced lay pastor. He has an elaborate system of ongoing training, evaluation, monthly reporting and accountability, all of which appear crucial to his system. It certainly works and is a good model.

Howard Stone describes a much simpler approach in *The Caring Church: A Guide for Lay Pastoral Care* (Harper and Row, 1983). He suggests eight training sessions and a service for commissioning lay pastoral caregivers. My personal preference is not for a crash course but an ongoing fellowship of pastors-in-ministry-and-in-training, focused on a monthly meeting of a minimum three hours' duration. One hour should be given to situational learning—discussing case studies that have arisen within their ministry or ones contrived by the equipping pastor. The second hour should be spent in prayer for one another and mutual support. The last hour should be dedicated to input by a resource person, possibly from outside the church, or to discussion of one of the many books that should be assigned as part of the ongoing equipping of lay pastors. (See the bibliography for further resources.) In a larger city where interdenominational resources are available, the equipping pastor can strategically direct some of the members of the group to more advanced resources, for example, seminars such as Premarital Preparation, The Skilled Helper, Marriage and Family Ministries Courses at a local seminary or Bible college.

Recognize Individual Gifting

Obviously not every lay pastor fits the mold of a "visitor," or a lay counselor or a person with a prayer healing ministry. Here is exactly where equipping lay pastors is more than delegating the pastoral office of the senior pastor. An equipping pastor with a large heart and a hunger to fan the coals of a person's growing edge will not try to get a group of ten or fifteen to fit into *his* expectations of what the church needs; he will welcome what God does.

Take Louise, for instance. When I think of Louise the words of the Servant in Isaiah 50:4 come to mind: "The Sovereign LORD has given me an instructed tongue [instructed in life], to know the word that sustains the weary." The best lay counselors are people who have experienced the Lord's healing touch and who, from that experiential base, can sustain others with their words and empathetic listening. Louise was involved in the New Life Community Church in Burnaby, British Columbia. Her pastors, David King and Murray Moerman, asked her to pray for people after the Sunday services and, to encourage her growing counseling ministry, sent her to a training seminar for lay counselors sponsored by a local Christian counseling center. In due course New Life Community Church started a lay counseling program with Louise as a volunteer staff person. Here is the substance of her invitation in the counseling program brochure. You can sense the authenticity in the invitation.

Dear Friends:

Welcome to our counseling service. We are a group of five counselors who are committed to helping you. We are here to listen, encourage, and pray with you concerning your individual, marriage, and family needs. Confidentiality is maintained amongst the team.

It takes courage and inner strength to commit yourself to counseling. I, myself, have gone through that process, so can affirm you in the step you're taking. As you and your counselor work together, you will both determine what you need to work on and what kind of counseling you need. We offer both clinical counseling (under supervision of Caretakers at Burnaby Christian Counselling Group) and prayer counseling for inner healing of past hurts.

In Christ's love,
Louise

But there is more to getting lay pastoring going than merely publishing a brochure.

Gain Congregational Ownership

This is a crucial step. Any pastor who wants to release lay pastoral care must patiently win the elders and/or the official board to the strategy. Their immediate response of "visiting and counseling are what we are paying the pastor(s) to do" must give way to the more biblical conviction that "God has given you to this church so that many of us can be equipped to do the work of the ministry" (Eph 4:11-12). This takes time, months and sometimes even years, but failure to gain agreement with the church leaders on an equipping strategy will have disastrous consequences. *Some* of the elders or board should be included in the training group if they are so gifted and inclined. But I do not encourage simply assuming that the senior lay leadership group should be the primary pastoral care team—their gifts may be in leadership, faith and administration rather than mercy, helps and wisdom.

Ownership should be gained at the congregational level as well. Preaching sermons on lay pastoral care, while a good thing, will not be as effective as modeling the commitment to it. When lay pastors are commissioned in a brief service within the Sunday service (see appendix B); when lay pastors, wearing a name tag that indicates that they are lay pastors, stand at the front and back after every service to help; when the pastor frequently mentions that lay pastors are visiting all the members of the church on a regular basis, the church leadership is making a powerful statement that "in this church pastoral care is provided by laypersons not just the pastor." Perhaps the most crucial moment in communicating the policy of the church comes when people ask, indeed sometimes demand, the pastor's time and ministry. The pastor must do pastoral work. But the pastor who yields to every invitation and every call for help will soon undo any equipping of lay pastors already accomplished.

Does it really work? Can the pastor share his own ministry with gifted and called laypersons and evoke pastoral ministries that even he or she does not have? Churches that follow this plan, each in their unique way, can testify that it does work. But more important, we must ask whether the old system of a one-person professional pastor has worked. Where it has worked there seems to be an unusual combination of a multi-talented individual with a high energy level. Many of these burn out, but the fact that all do not astonishes me. As John R. Mott first said, I would rather train ten persons to do the pastoral work than to do the work of ten persons![25]

LAY PASTORAL INTEREST QUESTIONNAIRE

Indicate below whether, if you have an opportunity, you would be drawn to one or many of these ministries. Do not let lack of training or affirmation of others keep you from indicating your strong or weak interest.

1. strongly interested
2. interested but mildly
3. can take it or leave it
4. would prefer not to spend time in this ministry
5. would definitely not want to be involved

(In the following ten pastoral ministries circle the response that is most appropriate for you.)

1. VISITATION—going to peoples' homes to welcome, solve problems, enfold, support, mediate and restore persons to the faith. Such shepherding is to be distinguished from being "rescuers" who place themselves in an indispensable relationship with the person in need.

1   2   3   4   5

2. PASTORAL COUNSELING—visiting with people usually in a one-to-one relationship to seek solutions for personal problems and to bring direction to the lives of people. What distinguishes pastoral counseling from psychological counseling is its prayerfulness and orientation to the Word of God. While empathetic listening and people-helping skills are crucial to this ministry, the pastoral counselor's goal is to allow the Word and Spirit to shape the pastoral relationship.

1   2   3   4   5

3. PRAYER COUNSELING (sometimes called inner healing)—praying in teams of two or three with persons suffering profound emotional hurts in order to actualize God's forgiveness, the healing of the emotions and restoration of the soul. In this ministry almost all the time together is spent in prayer.

1   2   3   4   5

4. MARRIAGE MINISTRIES—preparing people for marriage in Christ, helping couples experiencing marital stress, facilitating the enrichment of marriages, reconciling or conciliating alienated couples, caring for divorcing couples and divorcees.

1   2   3   4   5

5. FAMILY MINISTRY—facilitating the healthy development of families, helping families solve family problems, encouraging family spiritual formation and supporting families in pain.

1   2   3   4   5

6. SPIRITUAL FRIENDSHIP AND DIRECTION (sometimes called discipleship ministries)—being linked with people in a regular way to encourage individuals in their spiritual journey. This involves seeing that people in the church are truly converted, are being filled with the Spirit and have a genuine life in God. Some or all of the following matters are concerns of spiritual friends-directors: developing disciplines in prayer and Bible study, meditation, solitude, sabbath, healthy human relationships and personal emotional health, confession and appropriation of forgiveness, practicing the presence of God, releasing spiritual gifts. The ultimate goal of this ministry is not to become dependent on the friend (or director) but on God.

1   2   3   4   5

7. HEALING AND MINISTERING TO THE SICK—visiting and praying for the sick in hospital and home, engaging where needed in deliverance ministry where there is demonic bondage, and sustained prayer and loving support for the chronically ill who have not yet experienced God's healing and may not until the resurrection of their bodies.

1   2   3   4   5

8. MEDIATION AND RECONCILIATION—bringing together alienated persons to find ways of defusing conflicts, to identify the sources of the alienation and to work toward mutual respect and forgiveness.

1   2   3   4   5

9. DISCIPLINE—dealing with moral and spiritual problems in persons that affect the fellowship and relationships within the fellowship in such a way that persons are brought to repentance, reconciliation and restoration (rather than alienation from the community) and the health of the community is restored. Often this ministry requires pastoral interventions rather than merely responding to calls for help.

1   2   3   4   5

10. CARING FOR PEOPLE IN THE RITES OF PASSAGE—rejoicing with and ministering to families at the births, weddings, retirements and deaths. Ministry to the dying and their loved ones involves dealing with the stages of relinquishment, pastoral ministries at the point of death, healing the dying, assisting the grieving and conducting appropriate memorial or funeral services.

1   2   3   4   5

Four

Worship Leaders & Gift-Brokers

I confess to being a well-wisher of charismatic renewal. *This flam-*boyant and exciting movement has penetrated every conceivable branch of the church on every continent. It has also caused a lot of problems. But I would rather have all the problems of renewal than to try to keep new wine in the old bottles (Lk 5:36-39). This is especially true when it comes to worship.

This chapter is about equipping lay worship leaders. These thoughts may benefit those in highly formalized and liturgical churches, and others who prefer to remain at the perimeter of charismatic renewal. As its name suggests, charismatic renewal is concerned about gifts *(charisms)*. So I will include in this chapter some thoughts on spiritual gifts, especially the controversial ones. No renewal movement has a monopoly on kingdom life, but I think that the major contribution of charismatic renewal is not so much its emphasis on "gifts" as its emphasis on every-member worship.

Biblical Worship

In the church in which I grew up, worship was essentially a performance, magnificently given by organist, choir and ministers. The printed order of service was followed item by item. One wondered what would happen if, in answer to our prayer of invocation, God *did* show up in transcendent power or through the stirring of gifts in the congregation. While the service was in God's honor, the congregation was the first to benefit. In a consumer-oriented society this arrangement fits well. But biblical worship reverses the roles: God is the recipient of our praise; the congregation is the choir praising God; and the worship leader is like a choir director evoking and harmonizing the manifold contributions of the people. Let me develop these thoughts a little before turning to the crucial question of who should lead such worship.

Worship Is Responsive

Many people think that the task of a worship leader is to "work people up" to worship. But biblical worship has a responsive character and God is the chief initiator. God awakens our desire for worship, as he awakened in Adam a desire for his wife (Gen 2:18-23). This process is at work in the biblical vision of heaven. In the last book of the Bible, a mighty angel asks, "Who is worthy to break the seals [of the book of destiny] and open the scroll?" (Rev 5:2). When no one in heaven or on earth was found worthy, one of the heavenly elders pointed to the Lion of the tribe of Judah who was also the Lamb of God (5—6). The question was designed to evoke a response. The movement of the Christian life is from God-given grace to God-directed gratitude. Paul said that "in view of God's mercy . . . offer your bodies as living sacrifices" (Rom 12:1). In the tradition of my home church, eucharist, or the Lord's Supper, is celebrated every Sunday, as I believe it was in the primitive church.[1] The table is the center of worship, though the Lord's Supper does not constitute the circumference of worship. There is literally no entertainment value in it. It is pure response: gratitude or thanksgiving.

Worship Is Reverent

Biblical worship is inspired by the mercy of God. It is also directed
to the pleasure of God. A time of worship ends not with the arrogant
thought "Did I like the worship service?" but with the humble aware-
ness of God as the center of everything. Only thus can we be saved
from living eccentrically, at the mercy of every advertisement or
soothed by cultural placebos. So by acknowledging that God is God,
a seemingly useless activity which wastes precious time and money,
we are doing the most useful thing of all. If there is no center, there
is no circumference. If our lives are not heaven-penetrated, they will
be hell-threatened. If we lose our center, we will soon prove to be both
manipulated and manipulators.[2] In worship we actualize the reality
that "the Lord reigns" (Ps 93:1). With God in his place, we have found
our place as adoring creatures. Therefore humor and laughter are
appropriate acts of worship because they are ways of taking ourselves
less seriously. How different this is from much that passes for biblical
worship. Relational worship focuses on telling one another what God
means *to us.* Much "charismatic" worship focuses on the *experience*
of worship rather than the God who is beyond our experience; it often
seems directed toward the goal of a spiritual orgasm in a worship
service and seems bent on making this happen. Contemplative worship can gravitate to navel-gazing since it focuses on a person's unique
journey. Popular evangelical worship makes worship into a tool for
personal fulfillment: Worship and you will be healed, or worship and
you will prosper. But biblical worship starts and ends with the desire
to please God.

Worship Is Prophetic

I mentioned that worship is a useless activity. If we were to calculate
the value of the hours spent in the average congregation Sunday
morning, we must regard it as wasteful and expensive, especially
when a large part of the world is perishing for want of drinkable
water and good food. But there is a reason for such holy waste. The
writer of the letter to the Hebrews comments on the worship arrangements of the Old Covenant: the priesthood system, the sacrifices, the
festivals, the holy places and holy acts. He says, "They serve at a

sanctuary that is a copy and a shadow of what is in heaven" (8:5). The point of worship, whether the outward, symbolic Old Covenant arrangements or the inward, symbolic worship under the New Covenant, is simply this: It fits us for our life of worship in heaven. It serves an ultimate, prophetic purpose of meeting our need for God-centeredness, rather than catering to our compulsive need to be useful and productive.

This is manifestly the perspective of the Revelation, a book bathed in the atmosphere of worship. In this last book of the Bible, there is a balance of awe and intimacy, adoration and access, aesthetic sound and pregnant silence. The message of the Revelation is that "our Lord God Almighty reigns" (19:6), but there is an equally important message. It is that earthly worship should be modeled after heavenly worship (Rev 4—5) and that heavenly worship will be a continuum of our present life in the Spirit. By making us heavenly-minded, true worship renders us fit to live in this world with faith, hope and love. So we must refrain from spoiling congregational worship by bringing a utilitarian focus into it. It is meant to be rest, sabbath and an experience of playing heaven. More important than merely teaching us about heaven, worship is provisioning our imaginations to live a life of faith by means of an empowering vision. Transcendent worship empowers and envisions rather than teaches and instructs.

The story is told in the *Russian Primary Chronicle* of how Vladimir, prince of Kiev, while still a pagan in the tenth century, sent envoys to various countries to discover the true religion. After entering the Eastern Orthodox church of St. Sophia in Constantinople, they exclaimed, "We knew not whether we were in heaven or on earth, for surely there is no such splendor or beauty anywhere on earth. We cannot describe it to you: Only this we know, that God dwells there among men, and that their service surpasses the worship of all other places. For we cannot forget that beauty."[3] They noted three authentic signs of biblical worship—heavenly joy, the manifest presence of God and exquisite beauty—all within the tradition of a highly formalized liturgy and sacramental priesthood. We will explore these same realities in the context of free worship and every-member participation. In doing so, we must ask who is worthy to lead such worship and whether such leadership can be shared.

Worship Leaders: Conductors or First Violins?
I mentioned earlier that in biblical worship the congregation is the choir "performing" for God's pleasure and the worship leader is the conductor. Perhaps I overstated this contrast. In fact God leads his own worship service by moving with sovereign creativity through his Spirit in the hearts and spirits of his people, awakening our desire for himself. Just as Jesus does not delegate his headship of the church to the pastor or elders, so the Spirit does not delegate his envisioning and empowering role (Rev 1:10) to the human worship leader. Using the analogy of an orchestra, the worship leader is not so much the conductor as the first violin, who plays along with the rest but is responsible to set the tone for the whole orchestra. In my opinion this is a task wisely shared by the pastor with suitably gifted and trained laypersons. Here is why.

The Priesthood Factor
Under the Old Covenant, one tribe was assigned the priestly role of leading worship. Remarkably this was essentially a "lay" activity since men like Zechariah (Lk 1:5-10, 23) were self-supported ministers who did their annual duty in the temple.[4] But under the New Covenant all the believers are a community of priests (1 Pet 2:9-10; Rev 1:6). Priests touch people for God and touch God for people. However, under the fulfilled conditions of the New Covenant this is never an individual activity. "The priesthood of all believers," the watchword of the Reformation, is the priesthood of *all* believers. Together, the believers can touch the world for God and touch God for people. Sadly we observe that the Protestant rediscovery of this biblical truth became something like "You can be your own priest," especially under the individualism of the modern Western world. So when we approach one dimension of the ministry of the royal priesthood—the corporate worship of the Church in its gathered life—we must find a way to express the truth that all the believers together are the priests.

This changes the role of the worship leader. Instead of being either a representative or a vicarial priest, the worship leader is a servant-priest dedicated to evoking the corporate praise of the rest of the priests. This is a very demanding role since it will seem that a congregation is worshiping corporately when various individuals are "doing their own thing" through prayer, Scripture, prophecy and spontaneous expressions. But true worship is corporate, not merely the sum of the individual worship of all members when they are together. In practice this requires a combination of form and freedom, planned liturgy and open spontaneity. But above all, it requires leaders that can discern, usually with the help of elders, whether contributions from the body complement or compete with the corporate expression of the congregational priesthood.

The Giftedness Factor
So it is appropriate to speak of leading worship as a gift even though it is not named in the "gift lists" of the New Testament. All believers are priests, but only some priests have the God-given ability to facilitate the priestly worship ministry of the community.

A person gifted in worship leadership should have several of the following qualities:
- ☐ An obvious personal joy in worshiping God
- ☐ An equipping orientation through which they prize what others can contribute even more than their own contribution
- ☐ An ability to direct people Godward with an economy of words
- ☐ Discernment so that fleshly contributions can be distinguished from Spirit-prompted contributions
- ☐ A pastoral bearing that can gently correct the way things are moving while making people feel cared for and nurtured
- ☐ An appreciation of the crucial role music has in evoking praise (Worship leaders do not have to be musicians themselves, but they must want to work with them.)

In every congregation several such persons are usually waiting to be discovered. Evidence usually surfaces in small groups, on church retreats or during a devotional period at a church meeting. An equipping pastor can observe this, and in consultation with other church leaders, begin to introduce such persons into a team for leading Sunday morning worship. Sometimes the pastor is not even gifted to be a worship leader and yet is required to be the solo celebrant. That is sufficient reason to equip lay worship leaders. But there is another one that we should explore.

The Personality Factor

Don is a gifted worship leader in our community.[5] When he leads the congregational worship, people instinctively relax in the Spirit, knowing they will be neither badgered into making worship expressions nor left as a leaderless group. In contrast to some leaders who "play all the stops of the organ" by personally orchestrating the contributions of people, Don waits to see what God is doing in a service. When he stands up, he introduces the first two or three worship songs with an economy of words: "We are here to bless God. This song will enable us to express our love directly to God. We are not singing about him but to him."

In our church the teaching-preaching comes early in the service, usually after twenty minutes of preparatory worship. Then after the sermon come fifty minutes of responsive worship. This way worship is evoked by the Word of God, and the Lord's Table is the center, though not the circumference, of our worship. Worship is not a build-up for the sermon but the environment of the whole service. Thus, when the preaching is over, Don must pick up the mood of the message and gently invite people to express their response to God. He wants to bring the message home not merely to people but to God. Sometimes he will have to be ready to scrap or change what he had planned.

Few people realize that Don's worship services are thoroughly planned and prepared. He was careful to include praise, confession, forgiveness, Scripture reading and intercession, but it was not slapped together Saturday evening. In fact, when Don takes a worship service about once a month, he prepares all week for Sunday morning, making it part of his daily quiet time, meditating on the text to be expounded in the sermon and planning his theme around the subject of the sermon. Don meets on Thursday night with the music group—four instruments and three lead-singers—to practice the songs and to pray about the service. Since our church only occasionally has a soloist or a choir, Don wants to create the situation where the music group *and* the congregation join together as a choir to praise God. In this way, the congregation will become the performers and God will be the audience. Some weeks Don may put in as many hours preparing the worship service as the preacher did in preparing the sermon. But he loves doing it, and he especially loves it when he has been successful in getting himself out of the way so that people are left "seeing no man save Jesus only."

Jim, another member of our church, loves to preach and the people prize his gift. He is a strong and expressive person who loves to let scriptural truth be strained through his own personal experience. All true biblical preaching is incarnational. In a sense the preacher cannot help reveal himself or herself because, understood in the Hebraic way, the person comes out of the mouth. Jim doesn't mind this. In fact he rather welcomes the preaching task as a special way of personally relating to a congregation, influencing, challenging, loving, pastoring, admonishing. When Jim sees people getting "turned-on" in the sermon, all his creative juices flow. He loves it and the people love it too. Like Eric Liddell who felt God was pleased when he ran a race well, Jim feels that God is pleased when he preaches well. It is oral art, an experience of inspired creativity. But when Jim leads worship it is another matter.

Jim's worship leadership is like his preaching: expressive, exhortative, exciting and wordy. Jim finds it hard not to preach when he is leading worship. He wants to tell about his own experiences and to explain everything. He wants to create the response to his own planned worship service. Unlike Don, he is uncomfortable with silence, and when there is a long pause in the service during which people are invited to contribute a song, a Scripture, a word from the Lord or a prayer, Jim feels he must fill the silence with his own chatter.

Don and Jim represent two personality types. Don is evocative; Jim is provocative. Don is reflective; Jim is expressive. Don is excited by synergism within the congregation, the harmonizing of diverse gifts into a whole that is more than the sum of the parts; Jim is excited by the joy of communication. Don loves the prayer, the brooding and reflection that is preparatory to his worship leadership; Jim loves the study that is preparatory to his preaching. I admit that I have drawn this contrast a little sharply, but I have rarely met a good preacher who is, at the same time, a good worship leader and vice versa. That in itself is a powerful argument for equipping lay worship leaders.

The Equipping Environment

I have been exploring the reasons why a pastor should equip lay worship leaders and what kind of person makes a good worship leader. A conspiracy of equipping is implied in releasing biblical worship, because the worship leader equips the congregation to release the gifts God has given to this particular congregation, including the controversial ones of healing, prophecy, visions and words of knowledge. The more open we are to congregational participation the stronger and more discerning is the leadership that is needed.

But participatory worship implies even more about the environment. And the equipping pastor must be even more concerned to equip the church environmentally than to equip the individual lay worship leader. The learning environment is determined by a number of important factors, including verbal and nonverbal symbols and clues which tell a person whether their movement into ministry will be worthwhile and appreciated. In this chapter we are asking what it will take to release spiritual gifts in the context of public worship. Worship leaders are brokers of the gifts of the congregation, and they cannot fulfill their ministry if the gifts of the congregation are kept hidden or suppressed. So what is needed is an experimental climate.

An Experimental Climate

It is hard to imagine a church system more unproductive for equipping ministries than the one normally promoted. If by brilliant and creative human ingenuity a church structure were devised to *prevent* the development of gifts, it could hardly improve on what we have. Large groups of people assemble to hear one person or a very few exercise their gifts, while the majority ruminate, evaluate or otherwise passively listen. Seldom are people trusted with any concrete ministry

© Rob Portlock. Used by permission.

until they have proved themselves as Christians for several years. Little or nothing is expected of new Christians except that they study, listen and watch until they have grown mature. A high priority is placed on cognitive learning. Errors in doctrine or simple doctrinal immaturity are regarded as sufficient reason for people to do nothing except listen. Has an *enemy* designed this church structure?

Jesus' training methods contrast common church training today. Until perhaps two-and-a-half years of active service had passed, Peter appeared not to know that Jesus was the Christ, the Son of the living God (Mt 16:16). We have reason to think Peter had healed people and cast out demons long before he could adequately express in words his belief about Jesus. The unsuccessful attempt of the disciples to heal a convulsive child (Lk 9:40) suggest that they experimented *beyond* their faith and spirituality, not safely within it.

We should strive to create an atmosphere within a church in which spiritual gifts can be *tried out by anyone*. Obviously, trying out every gift in the worship service is not appropriate, but if there is not an experimental climate throughout the church people will be unlikely to express ministry in gathered worship. Even as I write this, I shrink a little because it sounds blatantly antispiritual, if not antisupernatural. But I ask myself this question: How did I develop the gift of teaching God manifests through me from time to time? By having the freedom to experiment with teaching. What then is needed for healthy experimentation?

Shortly after becoming a Christian, I was asked to give my testimony at a young people's meeting. I led what in those days was called a devotional. As time went on, people created situations in which I could minister to the body long before I dreamed that God had given me the gift of teaching. What might have happened if opportunity for experimentation had not been given? I wonder whether certain spiritual gifts may never have surfaced within me because I have never had an opportunity *to try*.

Awareness of Our Own Spiritual Desires

A crucial condition for experimentation is a healthy attitude toward motives. Often in Christian groups we assume that what *we* want to do is surely the exact opposite of what God wants us to do. But how can this *normally* be if we are "new creatures in Christ" and have the "mind of Christ"? Therefore, vital first steps are reflective prayer and meditation on the way God has made each of us and on the desires he has generated within us since our conversion. Certainly, not all our motivation is from God. But if Christ lives in us and if the old has passed away (2 Cor 5:17), *what we want to do for Christ will usually be an indication of a potential gift.*

We should expect that gifts will commonly be discovered in the fellowship through a combination of redeemed motivation and experimentation. Each of us is a fraction of Christ's body. Each has some special way of blessing the body. It is like our God to make us *want* that very ministry. That is why, in our house groups, we will wisely ask from time to time, "What do you like to do in the area of Christian service?"

A Climate of Expectation

"Nothing new will happen" is often a self-fulfilling prophecy. One component of faith is expectancy. Those of us who suffer from the "little faith" disease need constantly to ask: Is there something new God would do among us? Am I prepared to be surprised by God? Is there some new ministry of the Spirit in this situation which I am frankly not open to receiving or giving? Without desiring personal glory, am I open to being an instrument for praising God and loving his people through *any* of the spiritual gifts and with *all* the fruits of the Spirit?

Responsibility for Correction

The elders are responsible for shielding the church from the potential dangers of experimentation. If someone ministers in an unedifying way, the elders' task is to deal with it. This shelter of loving correction frees both the congregation and the experimenting believer from the inhibiting feeling that "if it goes wrong, the church will be destroyed." Plural leadership is essential to this shepherding role, since not every elder, nor any one pastor, has discernment concerning all gifts of ministry.

In our own fellowship, a worship leader can make eye contact with different elders and house leaders in response to somewhat questionable situations. And the leader knows that they can be trusted to discern when others might be unaware of all the dimensions of a certain ministry.

When charismatic renewal hit our church the elders decided that instead of merely endorsing it, or trying to shut it down, they would meet, study and pray until they could minister pastorally to the congregation. They then issued a pastoral statement to the congregation containing guidelines for the exercise of controversial gifts in the worship service. These are found in appendix C. Then the signs and wonders movement came to town. A few people influenced by John Wimber were bringing "words of knowledge" about the secrets of some members of our congregation. One particularly memorable Sunday someone read a letter from an out-of-town friend which called an unnamed former church leader to repentance for a secret adultery. As it turned out, the "word" was not a "word of knowledge." This ignited an internal controversy that could have been divisive if the elders had not once again ministered pastorally through study, prayer and teaching. The elders were convinced that it was better to take such risks than to quench the Spirit. The results of their study and guidelines for the pastoring of prophecy in the worship service are found in appendix D. The challenge to worship leaders is to regulate inappropriate offerings in such a way that it does not suffocate initiative. We must create an environment in which people are willing to try edifying the body and blessing the Lord in the public service.

Willingness to Try

One of my first steps in the area of prophecy was responding to a mental picture I was given while praying for a young woman. During a communion service, she had confessed at the altar rail her utter spiritual dryness and her desire to be refreshed in the Spirit. I prayed for her for a minute or two, and then God put in my mind a scene of rain falling on a desert. At first the sand was so dry that the falling rain had little noticeable effect. Only a slight dampness was apparent. But as the downpour continued, the land was being refreshed. Soon small rivulets and streams formed. Finally the streams became a river that fanned out to reach other dry areas of the desert.

Should I share this vision with my sister? I thought. What if it was not a prophecy but just a creation of my mind? (Can these two be totally and finally separated?) I had never prophesied formally. I decided to risk telling her what was in my spirit, knowing that this visual prophecy was in harmony with the great promises of Scripture. She received it as a message of encouragement from God. And that tender first experience encouraged *me* too. Not many weeks later I was able to share a similar prophecy-vision with the congregation, knowing that I was free to fail and free to share a word of encouragement even if it did not prove to be specially anointed.

Participatory Worship Services

Corporate worship must be restructured (or de-structured) to allow people to be surprised by God. Idols, whether physical or mental, never surprise because "they have mouths, but do not speak" (Ps 115:5). Those who worship such fixed and static conceptions of God become "like them" (Ps 115:8), rigid, stereotyped worshipers. Surely, one of the marks of God's personhood is his ability to surprise. But what room is there for surprise in the traditional worship service? Having the order of service laid out sometimes leaves little room for God.

On the other hand, the totally unstructured service, without order or visible leadership, can easily gravitate to the unacknowledged liturgy of habitual religion. As Peter Gillquist says: "There is nothing more distasteful during a public worship service than having three or four people scattered throughout a room doing 'something unique' to worship the Lord and embarrassing everyone else to tears."[6] We need a worship context that has sufficient order to draw the many private expressions of worship into a unity, but sufficient freedom to invite spontaneous participation. Paul's corrective word in Corinthians (1 Cor 14:27) assumes this balance.

The fellowship I serve uses a thematic approach to worship.[7] Within this context there are pauses and long silences during which the worship leader invites participation. Often a leading suggestion can both encourage people and bring a certain unity and order; for example: "The characteristic I appreciate about the Lord this morning is ..." At certain periods we invite people to share a word from Scripture or bring a word of exhortation to the fellowship. We avoid specific designations like "miraculous gifts" or "special gifts" in order to encourage people to share what they have, even if they are uncertain whether it falls into the category of a spiritual gift.

Three or four times a year we celebrate the Lord's Supper differently from our weekly practice. Teams of people, sometimes seven or eight couples, stand behind the specially arranged long table. As people come forward individually to receive the elements, those behind the table ask people if they have any specific need for prayer. In response to the incredible diversity of need, gifts of healing and prophecy are sometimes expressed. By involving nonelders in this praying ministry, a whole new group of people in the fellowship are exposed to the kind of prayer ministries usually experienced only by elders (Jas 5:14).

God needs no help in developing the gifts we have studied. He is sovereign. In great wisdom, *he* has distributed gifts in the body. *He* plants motivation in our heart to love him and serve each other through gift ministries. He is at work in us, and we labor, struggling with all *his* energy (Col 1:29). God doesn't need help. But we do, which is the reason he gave gifts designed to equip the body. In great wisdom, too, he designed the local church to encompass both common life and leadership training.

Our rigid structures, minimal expectations, habitual religion and shriveled spirituality are like the stone in front of Lazarus's grave. Only Jesus could bring him to life with his word. But the friends of Lazarus *could* help bring their friend to life—they could roll the stone away. And equipping lay worship leaders is one way of moving the stones away.[8]

The foregoing four chapters explored four ways to liberate the laity in the gathered phase of the church, using Bible learners and lay preachers, small group leaders, lay pastors and lay worship leaders. But the church is a rhythm of gathering and dispersion. If we liberate the laity only in the gathered phase and not in the dispersed phase, we will have missed the lion's share of every-member ministry. As Leonard Doohan, a Roman Catholic writer, notes, "Ironically with the increase of lay ministry in Church positions, we run the risk of diminishing lay transformation of the world."[9] The problem is with our definition of ministry.

Usually we define ministry as doing things for God which have an obvious religious or ecclesiastical character, like preaching, leading worship, teaching children, counseling, shepherding, discipling, welcoming, ushering and managing the church finances. Inside the church we understand ministry as edification, all the ways that we build one another up in the most holy faith. Outside the church we tend to define ministry almost exclusively as evangelism, winning the lost and presenting the gospel as widely as possible.

Evangelism and edification are obvious ways in which Christ can have a ministry through us. But is it ministry for a husband to listen empathetically to his wife or to have a special time with each of his children weekly? Is it ministry for a Christian in politics to invest sixty hours a week in her societal career for God, offering the touch of God among the principalities and powers that form the arena of her work? Is it ministry for an elementary-school teacher to revise the kindergarten curriculum, or for a mother to create a welcoming environment in the home? Are these legitimate ways of touching for God? Can Christian stockbrokers minister in their occupations, or must they relegate ministry exclusively to their neighborhood Bible study one night a week? Does God minister through us in the neighborhood, in the political arena, in the domestic context? Can we minister for him in our so-called secular jobs?

Unfortunately, we have largely relegated ministry to the layperson's discretionary hours, the five to ten hours he or she may give to churchwork each week. But the church is a rhythm of gathering and dispersion, like the gathering and dispersion of the blood from the heart in the human body. The only true picture of the church is a motion picture, perhaps even an angiogram, that marvelous videotape of the heart in motion, pumping.

We, the laity of God, declare his glory one hundred and sixty-eight hours each week. As Elton Trueblood said, "*Church-goer* is a vulgar ignorant word and should never be used. You cannot go to church, you *are* the church wherever you go."[10] If that is true then we are a half-liberated laity (including we clergy-laypersons) because we have a truncated definition of ministry. We have prioritized the gathered life of the church and relegated ministry to sacred things, sacerdotal roles and the sanctuary.

So we turn now to four ways to liberate the laity, this time in dispersion, as worker priests in the marketplace, neighborhood evangelists, marriage-builders and justice workers. We need a church full of ministers. Even more, we need a world full of missionaries.

Five

Worker-Priests in the Marketplace

The worst job I ever had was making rivets by hand. It was a mindless task but important experience in my life. For three months as a sixteen-year old, I cut off half-inch lengths of metal rod with a hacksaw. Then I put them into a metal die and banged the head on the rivet. I lost count in the thousands. It was better not to count, better to anticipate how long to the coffee break or the lunch break when I rewarded myself by reading magazines on photography, my hobby. Years later I would understand that in a dehumanized industry the strike, or threat to strike, is the chief form of leverage.

I realized week by week as I consumed Cokes and beat rivets, that the Sunday service I attended faithfully made no conscious attempt to bridge the church world and the work world. My family church catered to the carriage trade of Toronto so the ushers wore tuxedos.

The pastor preached passionately and eloquently, but only rarely was there a transcendent glimpse on the work world.

Every Sunday an older gentleman with a three-piece pin-striped suit sat in front of me. My dad, who was a company president, leaned over to me one Sunday during a lull in the service and informed me that this man had been released from prison a few months ago where he had been incarcerated for embezzling funds from the company he worked for. As an idealistic young teenager who had not yet become a Christian, I had very mixed feelings about this. I was thrilled that the church had accepted him back, "healed, restored, ransomed, forgiven" (as the hymnwriter put it). But I wondered if that whole sordid mess could have been avoided if our church had equipped worker-priests for the marketplace, rather than polished ushers for the carriage trade of Toronto. After all, I was spending two hours a week in the church building and forty hours in the workplace.

John Redekop, a Canadian social ethicist, observes:

> The average working Canadian spends some 88,000 hours on the job from the first day of full-time employment until the retirement celebration. Some people, such as physicians and farmers, accumulate more than 100,000 hours. . . . Most of us spend almost 40 percent of our waking time at work. In contrast, the average evangelical Canadian spends less than two percent, some 4,000 hours at church, during the working years. Yet the evangelical church puts most of its energies into the 4,000 hours; almost nothing into the world of work.[1]

Doing Theology from Below

Equipping worker-priests for the marketplace must start with pastors and lay church leaders listening to the questions people ask. Every pastor is built with the same basic anatomy: two ears and one mouth. Equipping works best if we do twice as much listening as speaking. Theology can be done "from below," starting with the questions people ask, or "from above," starting with the revealed Scriptures. Because we need not only a theology for the laity but one *by* the laity, we sometimes must start with the issues that the layperson presses on the Bible from experience in the workplace. And the first question is the one I kept asking that summer long ago.

Why Work?

Rivetmakers and human-robots on assembly lines, as well as people in countless office jobs, ask this question. Speaking to this, Daniel Yankelovich in *New Rules* observed that worker frustration in the United States shows up in poor product quality. He notes, "As recently as the late 70s, the University of Michigan reported that 27 percent of all American workers, more than one out of four, felt so ashamed of the quality of the products they were producing that they themselves would not want to buy them." Yankelovich describes workers today as struggling to revise the giving/getting compact in the workplace: For them to give unstintingly to the job, they demand in return important psychological incentives in addition to economic ones."[2] So "Why work?" is asked not only by the bored factory-worker but also by the fulfillment-oriented yuppie.

Narcissism, the cult of self-worship, demands that people find work which in the eyes of others has meaning.[3] For the homemaking mother, this is an especially relevant insight into contemporary North American culture; for it is precisely because others judge her work at home of little value, by the measure of financial remuneration or by public recognition, that she may answer the question "Why work for nothing?" by working outside the home. But is it right to work for greater and greater personal profit, especially in monetary terms? And does the Bible teach us *how* to live with the wealth we earn by being so diligent in fulfilling the so-called Protestant work ethic?

Is Profitability Wrong?

Laura just arrived back at work, having taken a half-hour off to pay a doctor's bill.[4] As she stepped into the elevator, Ron Strangway, one of the firm's partners, joined her. Ron asked how things were going. "I've just paid a doctor's bill of three hundred dollars . . . but begrudgingly," she answered. The story came out. Laura made an appointment with a specialist for her back problem. She waited three months. But at the end of the consultation he said he would call her in a few days when he had seen the X-rays. She called several times, left messages,

Drawing by H. Martin; © 1973 The New Yorker Magazine, Inc.

"My Protestant work ethic made me a bundle, but my Puritanical
guilt complex won't let me enjoy it."

and after considerable badgering, he returned the call with a request
for another consultation. He could find nothing wrong. But the bill
came anyway.

"That's free enterprise, capitalism, call it what you like," Ron said.
"We do the same thing. A client requests assistance. We prepare a
feasibility study. And whether it is feasible or not, we put a bill at the
client's door." Ron got off at the fourth floor, but Laura, when she sat
at her desk again, could not help feeling ripped off. Worst of all was
the thought that she herself was doing the same thing.

The tragedy is that few people bother even to ask the question.
Making money and American religion are so intertwined that the
television preachers who advertise a health-and-wealth gospel appeal
to a perceived national need and innate right in North American life.

This marriage of capitalism and Christianity was given a major push by a best-selling book, *The Man Nobody Knows,* written in 1924. Author Bruce Barton, claimed that Jesus was the founder of modern business. Taking the theme text "Wist ye not that I must be about my Father's business?" Barton turned Jesus' call to service in Mk 10:43-44 upside-down by making self-sacrificing service the key to success. Barton outlined Jesus' business philosophy: "(1) Whoever will be greater must render great service. (2) Whoever will find himself at the top must be willing to lose himself at the bottom. (3) The big rewards come to those who travel the second, undemanded mile."[5]

Barton's daring picture of Jesus as the master advertisement specialist and business promoter was followed by a spate of books and articles which marry Christian pragmatism to the American way of profit.[6] While many believe this is the Protestant work ethic in action, it is really a perversion of Puritanism. American pragmatism puts man at the center, using God to facilitate the development of human potential. Puritanism, especially in its original explanation of the doctrine of calling, puts God in the center and refers all human activity to the desire to please and serve God. This turns out to be a crucial insight. Busyness and boredom are symptoms of the same disease of self-centeredness. People who are either compulsively busy or chronically bored do not have God at the center. So the question of profitability stirs us to deep reflection about the ultimate purpose of work. But there are other questions as well.

Is the System Demonic?

An example from another culture may serve to illuminate the probing question asked both by those who work from within the capitalistic system and outside. Now that free enterprise is making inroads within Soviet society, we may see ourselves in a different light by observing their faltering first steps. We may also understand the special equipping challenges facing the leaders of Soviet churches who want to equip worker-priests for the marketplace and not merely lay pastors for the gathered life.

A local newspaper columnist reports that on his recent visit to Moscow he saw a man selling light bulbs on a rickety card table

alongside one of the ring roads surrounding the capital. Knowing that
light bulbs were in short supply he was especially interested, and even
more so when he discovered they were being sold for five kopecks—
a few cents. When he realized they were all burned out, and this man
was still doing a brisk business, his curiosity demanded an interview.
The man explained that he was selling light bulbs to people who
worked in state offices, where bulbs were not rationed. His customers
would take a burned-out one to their office, replace the good one with
the dud, and then demand the caretaker replace the burned-out bulb.
The office worker would then take the good bulb home. The man at
the card table explained, with obvious pride, "Everybody gets light
bulb and I make a five-kopeck profit. Is this not good business?"[7]

In a country where entrepreneurial business is seldom more than
finding a way to "beat the system," it will take a vocational conversion
for Christians to do business for God's glory. But it also takes vocational conversion in the West, because there is no uncomplicated way
to do business or to develop a professional practice. What the average
Christian realizes today, however dimly, is that he or she is not in
charge of his or her own circumstances. The "authorities and powers"
(Eph 6:11-12) Paul mentioned are a daily reality. The small business-
person has very little freedom and often feels that survival is a matter
of daily spiritual warfare.

But perhaps it is even harder working for a large multinational
corporation which seems to have taken on a life of its own—intransigent, resistant to change, sometimes making idolatrous demands.
Some of the most progressive firms, especially in high-tech fields, are
more like a monastic order than a company. They demand unspoken
vows equivalent to the monastic vows of chastity, stability (living in
one place), poverty and obedience. Some openly require the renunci-
ation of normal family life, commitment to move anywhere the company requires (thus turning the vow of stability inside out), obedience
to the company hierarchy, all for the gain of large incomes and challenging assignments (One is allowed not to take the vow of poverty!).

As a Christian, Peter struggles with the system working in a non-
Christian law firm. He is becoming increasingly disillusioned with the
adversarial system. The reasons he gives are threefold. First, rather

than reconciling the parties, litigation tends to aggravate the tensions between them. Second, the expense of going to trial favors the wealthy who can wear down impecunious opposition into a favorable settlement by prolonging pre-trial procedures. The expenses may even preclude litigation altogether. Finally, the adversarial system requires one to promote the client's case without regard to its merits; this sometimes implicates a lawyer in achieving unjust results.

As Peter pondered the alternatives he felt he had some options: He could play the game, accepting the personal compromises and tensions inevitably involved, while seeking to minimize his culpability. Or, he could join a Christian firm in which he could refuse cases he did not feel morally comfortable with. As a final option he could conclude that litigation is not an area for Christians, and they should enter another area of law or establish a mediation center for alternatives to the court system. One option that did not seem open to Peter was to leave law and go into the professional ministry. His pastor friends warned him that they, too, had to deal with "the principalities and powers" in the institutional church, and not all their decisions were clean-cut! Peter's problem raises another question.

How Can I Work in Morally Grey Areas?
Gene runs a card shop that is a franchised dealer for a world-class card supplier. He has signed a loyalty agreement with them. Halloween has become the fastest growing "holiday" season, in terms of sales. To respond to this, the supplier has increased the number of products offered each year and expects these products to be prominently displayed in stores. Most of the products offered are "in good taste" socially, with a few exceptions. But the exceptions are those which portray witches and evil spirits.

Gene had become a Christian in the last few years. He bought the store from his father (who is not a Christian), who had also bought the store from his father. The conflict between Halloween and Christian faith had never been an issue in the owner's life until he became a Christian, and, of course, it had never been an issue with his father.

The conflict now raises itself in two ways. First of all, he and his wife just had their first baby. They both felt that they would not celebrate Halloween with their children, yet Halloween continues to be a profitable season at the store.

Secondly, some people in the church he attends take a strong stand against Halloween. He feels judged by people who know very little of his situation and the dilemma he faces. His friend who owns a Christian bookstore offers little in the way of consolation or understanding. He struggles with the confused feelings of defensiveness, on the one hand, and a personal repulsion of Halloween, on the other.

Gene made an appointment this afternoon with his pastor, saying over the phone that he was confused and depressed. How should Gene respond to his situation? The equipping pastor must be ready to discuss this question and at least one more.

What Makes a Person's Work Christian?

Is it the Christian character of the work, such as preaching, selling Christian books or doing pastoral visitation? Is it that a genuine need is being met, as in the case of a doctor or social worker? Is it the intent of working as though Jesus were one's employer?

A friend of mine suggested that if every Christian in the market-place said nothing about Jesus out loud but worked for Jesus in his heart and let the quality of his life and work speak for his Lord, there could be a greater spread of the faith than through the noisy Christians who do shoddy work but preach well. Sadly, I agree with him. Christians are often poor workers. And I have come to believe that it stems from a deep dichotomy within them. They feel that really important work is witnessing, preaching, pastoral care, teaching Sunday school and being a local church elder, while pushing pieces of paper across a desk or answering the telephone is of no eternal value and of little interest to God.

This prioritizing of "ministry" over "work" is now a fatal disease in Western Christianity. The work of the ministry has triumphed over the ministry of work. Careers and jobs are listed in the minds of believers from top to bottom in a scale of holiness and eternal relevance: missionaries and pastors on the top and stockbrokers on the bottom. As Richard Broholm says, "More and more I am convinced that a fundamental reason why so many Christians find it hard to initiate and sustain a ministry in their work place is that they really do not believe that they are, in fact, called to ministry. In spite of sermons on the 'priesthood of all believers' and admonitions to 'live your faith in your daily work,' the organizational and liturgical practices of the church continue to reinforce the assumption that there is no valid ministry outside the organizational church."[8] So the problem is deeper than mere program. Worker-priests need a theology and spirituality of work. That means that pastor and people must work together in teaching and learning a spiritual theology of work. Once more it must be a gracious conspiracy of pastor and people since the pastor does not have all the answers. And the worker-priests do not have all the questions!

Doing Theology from Above

Thus far in the chapter we have been doing theology "from below," starting with the questions people ask. But we can never establish a truly Christian theology of work simply by reflecting on our own questions, because apart from divine revelation we cannot make sense out of our lives. So in forming a biblical theology of work, we must humbly come to God to learn what issues he raises by speaking into our existence. Here are ten affirmations about work in the Bible.

1. *Work is a good gift from God* (Gen 1:26-31; 2:15). It is a blessing because it enables us to be co-creators with God who also "works." Therefore it has the potential of being an act of worship to God and a way of gaining spiritual depth. As Dietrich Bonhoeffer said so insightfully, work in the world *takes us out of ourselves.*[9] It does both the world and us good. Even routine jobs like garbage collection, morally difficult jobs like being a police officer, and seemingly useless jobs like writing poems or playing the oboe, serve a fundamental purpose. A passage from the Apocryphal book Ecclesiasticus says that such jobs "keep stable the fabric of the world." The whole passage is worth quoting:

> How can he become wise who handles the plow ... who drives oxen and is occupied with their work, and whose talk is about bulls? He sets his heart on plowing furrows, and he is careful about fodder for his heifers. So too is every craftsman and master workman who

labors by night as well as by day; those who cut the signets of seals, each is diligent in making a great variety; he sets his heart on painting a lifelike image, and he is careful to finish his work. So too is the smith sitting by the anvil, intent upon his handiwork in iron; the breath of the fire melts his flesh, and he wastes away in the heat of the furnace; he inclines his ear to the sound of the hammer, and his eyes are on the patter of the object. He sets his heart on finishing his handiwork, and he is careful to complete its decoration. So too is the potter sitting at his work and turning the wheel with his feet; he is always deeply concerned over this world. . . . He molds the clay with his arm and makes it pliable with his feet; he sets his heart to finish the glazing, and he is careful to clean the furnace. All these rely upon their hands, and each is skillful in this own work. Without them a city cannot be established, and men can neither sojourn nor live there. . . . *They keep stable the fabric of the world, and their prayer is in the practice of their trade.* (Ecclus 38:25-32, 34, emphasis mine)

2. *Work is never merely remunerated employment,* and not merely the creation-directed portion of our human task. According to the first three chapters of Genesis, every person has three full-time jobs: communion with God (Gen 1:26-31; 3:9; 3:13), community building with neighbor and family (Gen 1:26; 2:18) and co-creating with God (1:26-28; 2:15). Both male and female are called to all aspects of human work: the spiritual (enriching fellowship with God); the relational (enriching our cohumanity); the corporate (engaging in community building with family, church and society); and giving leadership to the created order under the leadership of God himself. In other words, the male is not càlled to dominating the world and the female, to home-making.

3. *All three dimensions of work were distorted through humanity's revolt,* resulting in alienation from God, the shattering of community, and the rape of the earth instead of co-creativity. Work became cursed through people's sin (Gen 3:17). Work itself became a *temptation,* and has been since the great revolt in the Garden of Eden. When people try to establish their identity and purpose in life through their daily work, work can even become an *idol.* This may especially tempt those

in challenging professions. Workaholism, an addiction to work, reveals just as much about work as it does the individual worker. Work creates the illusion that it can satisfy our deepest needs. Work seems to meet ultimate needs by giving us status (I am an engineer), by giving us measurable values for ourselves (My salary was raised last year twenty per cent.) and by giving us the potential of gain, either the approval of others or power over them (I was promoted to general manager). Idolatry is simply making something one's ultimate concern other than the One who is ultimate. Work easily fits into this mold. So when unemployment hits, or underemployment, the idol fails us. Only a mixed life of reflection and engagement can help those of us in demanding professions to remain amateurs who work for love rather than work-worshipers.

But while work has been cursed it is now redeemed, at least partially, by Christ in this life. The curse may be substantially reversed. Liberated from both "owning" creation, or worshiping it (the two extremes), the redeemed human steward is called to work not only at community building but at restoring the broken creation. Men and women in Christ work on the problems of pollution, food distribution, injustice, genetic engineering and the proliferation of violence and weaponry, knowing that this work is ministry and holy. In the short run this work may seem unsuccessful, but in the long run it will be gloriously successful while the believer cooperates with what Christ wants to do in renewing all creation. When Paul said, "Your labor in the Lord is not in vain" (1 Cor 15:58) he was not referring exclusively to church work, but work done for God in the church or world. Undoubtedly much Christian service will, in the last day, be burned as hay and stubble, and much so-called secular work done in faith will last!

4. *Work is part of our calling.* The New Testament points to a broad fulfillment of the Old Testament in proclaiming the new creation in Christ and, above all, in its treatment of calling or vocation. But once again work is a temptation. Earlier we saw how work can be an idol. Now we see how work may be viewed *merely as an instrument* to accomplish something. The idea of vocation or calling is that we are summoned by another—by God himself—to a life lived for his pur-

poses. An instrumental view of work takes too low a view, and the church has unwittingly aided and abetted that view. For instance, Thomas Aquinas is often quoted as proposing four purposes for work: the acquisition of necessary livelihood, the avoidance of the capital sin of idleness, the subjugation of the rebellious flesh by asceticism and the making possible of almsgiving through the abundance of material goods.[10] Thus understood, work has a penitential and atoning function through which the ordinary Christian takes up a cross in the world. But this view does not envision work as part of our calling to live for God and his kingdom. Few modern Christians would elaborate this view as negatively as Thomas Aquinas, but the same division between "having to work" and "doing what one really wants to" exists today. This leads to the next crucial statement.

5. *Vocation (what we are called to do) and avocation (what we do for love) were meant to be one.* The average person works at an idiot job making money to spend on the experiences he or she really wants: hobbies, sports, travel,. and other leisure activities. "Vocation" is the dread necessity; "avocation" is what one does out of love. But God intended that vocation and avocation be one, all for love so making us true amateurs. This was beautifully expressed by Robert Frost in one stanza of his poem "Two Tramps in Mud Time."[11]

Frost wrote that he wanted to unite his avocation and his vocation, just as "two eyes make one in sight." Only so, he suggested, would work be filled with passion and meaning. When "love and need" are combined, "work is play for mortal stakes" and we labor for the sake of heaven and the future.

6. *The dichotomy of evangelism and social justice is not only unfortunate but sinful!* The gospel restores people to the task of being human; it does not make them religious. While the center of the church's mission must always be the redemption of persons, the circumference involves all of life in this world. Many Christians think their workplace is mainly a location for witnessing. But both evangelism and social action relate to the ministry of work. Unfortunately the Greek word *dikaios* is translated by two English words, "righteousness" and "justice," thus seducing Christians into separating righteousness as an inward and spiritual state from righteousness as

a societal, social and political program. It is incorrect to say the Old Testament teaches the "creation mandate" (dominion) which is now superseded by the "new creation mandate" of Matthew 28:18-20 (evangelism). What Christ equips us to do is to restore the three full-time jobs to God's glory: communion, community building and co-creativity. Fortunately in many Third-World countries evangelical Christians have somehow avoided our tedious debates about evangelism and social justice and simply do both!

7. *Christ's and the Christian's ministry is both to persons and to structures.* The human task of imaging God's rule on earth includes not only nature but culture and all of the structures of human society. What are called "authorities," "powers," "dominions" and "thrones" (Rom 8:38; Eph 1:21; 3:10; 6:12; Col 2:10) describe the structures and ordered ways God created the world, the invisible background of our lives. These are not the result of the Fall but are created by Christ (Col 1:16) and for him, though they are now coopted or colonized by Satan (Eph 6:10-12). We cannot escape struggling with these vanquished but still rebellious powers, not even in so-called Christian work.

8. *There is no arena, however demonic, to which one cannot be called by God to minister.* By his death and resurrection, Christ has disarmed, made a public spectacle of, and triumphed over the powers (Col 2:15). They are like chained beasts kicking themselves to death. No place is off-limits to Christians responding to the call of God and going in the name of Christ.

9. *There is no hierarchy of ministries or services to be rendered by our work.* Hendrik Kraemer puts it this way: "All members of the *ecclesia* have in principle the same calling, responsibility and dignity, have their part in the apostolic and ministerial nature and calling of the church."[12] Ministry is work and work is ministry for the Christian. William Tyndale, the English Reformer, was considered heretical and executed for teaching, among other things, that "there is no work better than another to please God; to pour water, to wash dishes, to be a souter [cobbler], or an apostle, all is one; to wash dishes and to preach is all one, as touching the deed, to please God."[13] That is not simply saying that Luther's dairy-maid was called to milk cows[14] but

that the call to live for God and his kingdom may come to us anywhere
and be expressed anywhere (1 Cor 7:17, 20).

If this is true, supported Christian ministry is not the vocation of
vocations (as Calvin said) but merely one way of responding to the
single call that comes to all (Eph 4:1). Most expositions about ministry
are magnetically attracted to the supreme place of the ordained professional minister as the minister-par-excellence. It is small wonder
that laypersons aspiring to ministry attempt to become amateur cler-
gypersons.

10. *What pleases God in our work is faith, hope and love.* People like
Laura, Peter and Gene ask what pleases God in their daily work.
Their questions are probing. Does the religious character of what they
do please God—especially if they have the privilege of being a pastor
or a missionary? Or does the excellence of their work? Is God pleased
with the appropriateness of the task to the worker? Or with the
meeting of a genuine human need by one's labor (1 Thess 4:11-12)?
Or with being able to give to the poor out of one's excess (Eph 4:28)?
Is God primarily pleased by our having good relationships with one's
coworkers? Or is God pleased when we treat Jesus as our employer
(Col 3:23)?

Paul hints profoundly about the answer to this final question in
1 Thessalonians 1:3. "We continually remember before our God and
Father your work produced by faith, your labor prompted by love, and
your endurance inspired by hope in our Lord Jesus Christ." His emphasis on faith, hope and love—all *internal* fruits of the Spirit—is
exactly what we need because a driven person may appear on the
outside much the same as a called person. But on the inside there is
a huge difference.

"Work produced by faith" means that we consciously desire in our
work, whatever it is, to please God. In contrast, even a sermon can
be delivered for self-glory, and, like the moneychangers in the temple,
we pastors can take a percentage of others' worship of God. Working
by faith means *not* seeing the results of what we do, but doing it for
God and learning, perhaps long afterwards on the great day, that we
did it to him.

Paul also refers to "labor prompted by love." One way of laboring in love is to find work we love doing. But then we may find ourselves overworking because we love doing so many things. We may even lust for our work! We will labor in love when we love the people we are doing it for—the primary recipients, our family, or the poor, all of whom benefit from the proceeds. We will labor in love when we love the people we work with, thus being delivered from destructive competitiveness and damaging comparisons. But ultimately work must be suffused with empowering gratitude to God that overflows in love— love for God, love from God and the love of God.

"Endurance inspired by hope" is the climax, not the anticlimax, of 1 Thessalonians 1:3 because we need hope more than we need love. When we struggle with the seeming resultlessness of what we do, we need an empowering vision of the New Jerusalem and the consummation of the kingdom that is "here" and also "not yet." Our failures in nerve in the work place are in reality failures in imagination. We cannot see (except by faith, love and hope) where we are going. Hope involves rejecting our analysis of the status quo in favor of a view that rests on the sovereignty of our good God, who will bring the whole human story to a worthy end, marketplace and all!

Having looked then at the theology we do "from below" and "from above," we must now consider how to do this theology as a church.

Doing Lay Theology Together

The weakest link in the gathered services of the church surely is the preparation for re-entry into the world. Sunday is too separated from Monday. The work of the ministry has priority over the ministry of work. And, as William Diehl so wisely observed, nowhere is the separation of Sunday and Monday more pronounced than in the different spiritualities of Sunday and Monday: Sunday is all about salvation by grace through faith; Monday is all about salvation by works and achievement.[15] So I wish now to go beyond the cursory suggestions I made about equipping for the marketplace in *Liberating the Laity*.

Systemic Equipping

As we saw in the introduction, the church needs to be equipped even more than the individual member. Therefore, the church as a system must prize the value of the church member in the marketplace, even as much as the returned missionary with his awe-inspiring slides and stories. Here are some ideas, most of them tried and proven in more than one church.

☐ *Interviewing Marketplace Ministers.* Some do this with a different member each week as part of the service. This can be brief (from three to five minutes), but profoundly influential. A careful selection of members—those who believe God has called them to the market-place—and of questions that bring out the interpretive insights contained above will do more than many sermons on the theology of work. William Diehl's three questions would be excellent starters: What is the nature of your work? What kind of problems do you encounter and what decisions do you have to make? How do you relate your faith to these problems and decisions?[16] Churches which make this a weekly part of their service bring the dispersed life into the gathered life. A brief prayer of blessing for the person who shares will focus congregational support on worker-priests.

☐ *Intercessory Prayers for Members in the Marketplace.* The "pastoral prayer" or its equivalent is a crucial communication dimension. We tell what and who we love by our prayers! So it is crucial, if we love the world the way God does (Jn 3:16), that we pray for those who are struggling and hoping in the marketplace.

☐ *Lay Marketplace Preachers.* We've devoted a whole chapter to equipping lay preachers. Let me emphasize that the occasional involvement of a marketplace minister in the pulpit will have a multiple impact. When Dr. Bert Cameron brings a sermon in our congregation, often just having visited the hospital where he is in charge of a renal unit, a profound message is being given just by *his* giving it! It is a case of the metamessage being more important than the message. He brings perspectives from the world of medicine that few pastors can. His lack of expertise in preaching is not only forgiven but hardly noticed because of his powerful incarnational ministry. But let me make a warning here. Church ministry is usually so powerfully reinforcing, through the social approval process, that worker-priests who preach helpfully will be tempted to become regular lay preachers and to neglect the first arena in which God has called them to serve. That may not be best for them or the kingdom.

□ *Ordination of Worker-Priests.* This is a touchy question. But I have concluded that ordination as practiced in mainline churches has historical validity but very shaky biblical validity. The essence of the problem is not whether there should be such a thing as ordination, but who should be ordained. In a fine historical, exegetical and theological study of ordination, Vancouver scholar Marjorie Warkentin concludes that "the vocabulary of New Testament leadership permits no pyramidal forms, it is the language of horizontal relationships. . . . Ordination can have no function in such a system, for it sets up barriers where none should exist, that is, between one Christian and another and hinders the mutual service by which the church is edified."[17]

I believe there is a place for ordination. But if we are convinced that ministers who are fully supported by the church should be commissioned, then we must also find some way to ordain lay ministers. The Bible bears witness to people being commissioned to ministries to which God has called them (Acts 13:1-2). According to Ephesians 4:1 and 1 Corinthians 7:17-20 every believer is called, not just the professional minister. While it is appropriate for churches and denominations to set apart, with the laying on of hands, a leader who equips the saints (Eph 4:11-12), it seems equally appropriate to me, that others should be ordained. But I have some important provisos.

First, we should not ordain indiscriminately! Paul tells Timothy not to lay hands hastily on anyone (1 Tim 5:22). Just as no one should be ordained to pastoral ministry or to eldership without a proven ministry in the home (1 Tim 3:1-13) and the church, so no one should be commissioned by the congregation to a mission in the workplace without a long period of apprenticeship. We should single out those who have a proven sense of call over a long period of time and give them the same recognition we do to pastors and overseas missionaries. Further, it is important that any church considering this should have the long-term view. To ordain one or two, and then to give up would be a serious mistake.

James Garlow in *Partners in Ministry* gives us a pattern for a lay commissioning service which is found in appendix E.

Congregational Study and Learning

Since work occupies about one-third of a person's life and one-half of his or her waking hours, it is essential that the Word of God be brought to bear on this crucial subject. Here are some ways to do it:

□ A series of sermons can be preached on the theology of work or the covenant mandate developed above.

□ An adult elective in the Sunday school can explore the various biblical passages on work. One useful study guide for this is the one I coauthored with Gerry Schoberg: *Satisfying Work: Christian Living from Nine to Five*.[18] It contains thirteen inductive Bible studies from Genesis to Revelation on the subject of work.

□ One of the best ways to bring marketplace perspectives into the gathered life of the church is to develop an integrated Bible study about work. The pattern is very simple and reinforcing. Each week small groups in the church study a passage on work (perhaps using the study guide *Satisfying Work*), then on Sunday the pastor preaches *from the same passage*. Contrary to what people commonly fear, these do not usually overlap. We often learn more this way than by having a different theme for each learning opportunity the church offers during the week. This was developed more completely in chapter one.

□ Nelvin Vos suggests a series of questions that can form the basis of a marketplace ministry discussion in a small group or Bible study class: (1) Describe your main daily activity—what you do and where you do it. (2) About how many persons do you meet in the average day? (3) About how many of these persons do you "minister" to in as broad or narrow a sense as you wish. (4) How do you minister to these persons? (5) List at least three kinds of decisions you make in your daily activity. (6) Does your Christian faith affect your decisions? How? (7) How could you be better equipped and supported in your ministry in the world?[19]

□ Pastors can work through case studies with small groups of marketplace ministers. The stories of Laura, Peter and Gene are samples of case studies that can help us crack open marketplace issues. A good way to approach such case studies is to get the facts. Ask clarifying questions, identify the issues, ask what is at stake if various approaches are taken, and then discover what insights and direction the

Bible can bring to the persons involved.

☐ An ethics course makes a great adult elective in the church school. In this chapter's bibliography I have listed a number of appropriate books on this subject.

Networking in the Marketplace

A Toronto doctor recently said, "I have thrown away my books on moral theology. Now I just read my Bible, pray for the leading of the Spirit and trust my intuition." On one hand I see this as a magnificent confession of faith. But, on the other hand, I wish that he were not alone. A group of laypersons in his church could gather with their pastor and work through case studies with Scripture, prayer and secondary sources. Worker-priests need one another, especially in the grey areas!

Many believers find that a noon-hour or an early morning meeting with other Christians is a major resource for living out their lives to God's glory in the marketplace. Some local churches are large enough to have several members in one geographical location, thus rationalizing a local church network. The pastor of this church is fortunate, indeed, if he or she is invited to be a part of this group. Perhaps his or her greatest ministry is simply listening and asking questions, since people tend to turn to the pastor for definitive answers and, thus, short-circuit the essential learning process. Business people can help equip their pastors by inviting them to join a business group.

When several churches have worker-priests in the same area, they have good reason to join together in an inter-church network for support and fellowship. The temptation is that these groups will merely study the Bible and pray (I find these words hard to write) when they need to bring the real and hard questions of their work experience to the light of God's Word and the fellowship of believers.

Regent College, Vancouver,[20] where I am academic dean, offers a conference once a year on Christians in the Marketplace. Along with colleges like New College for Advanced Christian Studies in Berkeley, California, and the Institute of Christian Studies in Toronto, Regent College offers courses on Christianity and the Economic Order and other topics of crucial importance to people in the marketplace.

Our city, like many others, has a marketplace chaplain who ministers full-time to the downtown core. In addition, a splendid organization run by the Mennonites provides resources for people. Mennonite Economic Development Associates (MEDA) is an organization committed to honoring God in the marketplace. Its official purpose reads like a noble mission statement: "As Christians in business our mission is to honor God in the world of work and economics by extending his reign to all our activities. With Jesus as Lord of the marketplace, our task is to love, serve, preach and heal. We use our faith, skills and resources to correct inequities, work toward economic justice, seek righteousness, bring hope where there is not hope, and make all things new."[21] InterVarsity Christian Fellowship also runs a Marketplace Ministry which provides crucial guidance to students who want to serve God but are not sure how. We will briefly look at the matter of vocational guidance now.

Vocational Counseling

The pastor of a church often is approached for vocational counseling. One of the most sensitive questions he faces from a young person is, Should I go into the professional ministry?

We have many models of excellent preachers, missionaries and pastors. What we need today, and only the church can provide this, are models of people in the marketplace who have been transformed by Christ and *stayed where they are.* Too often they become circuit-riding preachers and tell their "punch press to pulpit" stories. Anne Rowthorn writes that "an essential step in the recovery of an appropriate spirituality for all persons is to look around and recognize in each other and in every aspect of human activity the ways in which Jesus is manifested, made known and followed."[22] Then she quotes the intertestamental book of Ecclesiasticus (38:25-32, 34), and reflects on all the modern worker-priests who minister in their work on farms, in homes and in cities: "All these rely on their hands, and each is skillful in his own work. Without them a city cannot be established, and men cannot sojourn nor live there.... They keep stable the fabric of the world, and their prayer is the practice of their trade."

Laura, the woman with the doctor's bill mentioned earlier in the chapter, came to accept the challenge of working for profit in a Christian way. She learned to do battle with greed within herself and the seduction of the system outside. Peter left law for awhile to deepen his faith by studying at Regent College. There he gained the beginnings of a Christian mind. After a year of Christian studies, he returned to law, being fully convinced that he could be there for God, moral ambiguities and all. Gene resisted the temptation to leave the store and go into a Christian service career. His pastor helped him to network with other Christian retailers. He found a way to be "in" the complicated world of retail sales without being "of" it. Now he sees his business as a mission.

Work cannot be a mission unless, as Dorothy Sayers said, "one really gets into one's work,"[23] doing it heartily with all one's might as a ministry, *for the sake of the work itself,* which is worth doing for its own sake even if it is not a people-helping job. This is not likely to happen unless we develop a contemplative lifestyle with reflection on the meaning of what we do. As Alfons Auer says, "Meditation will . . . enable a person in the technological world to discover the sense of *transparency in worldly matters* over and above the rational realization of their function."[24] It is just this "transparency" that makes daily work a ministry of faith, hope and love rather than mere labor or a disappointing idol. If that were to happen by preaching a spirituality of work then the work Christians perform would simultaneously be prayer and witness. And as the Russian Orthodox theologian Berdyaev said, Easter, which is the eighth day of creation, would be prolonged indefinitely as Christians participate in the ongoing life of Christ's risen life in the world. With the single eye Christians would love God from nine to five.

Six

Neighborhood Evangelists
By Michael Green

I f the leaders of local churches are really serious about liberating the lay people in the congregation for the difficult, challenging, and yet intensely rewarding task of spreading the good news in their neighborhood, there are a number of important steps to take.

They Must Get the Vision
One of the most fundamental of all New Testament truths for the church is this. All, not some, are called to be his ministers. There is no two-class travel for passengers on the Christian train: class one for pastors and class two for the rest. The New Testament knows of no Christians who are not ministers and witnesses. The worship of God and the witness to the world are both the prerogative and the responsibility of the *whole* church.

Anybody moderately at home in the literature of the New Testament knows this to be the case. It is beyond dispute. And yet almost every branch of the Christian church, whatever their denomination and theoretical beliefs, has made precisely that division between pastor and people. As a result, the congregations, no matter what their denomination, are instinctively persuaded that evangelism, along with other "church" activities, is the job of the pastor: "This, after all, is what we pay him or her for."

That attitude is fatal to dynamic Christianity. And pastors must realize it. If they want to go it alone, alone they will be. And the neighborhood will not be evangelized. They have to understand and passionately believe that the spreading of the good news is the task of all the members of the congregation.

They Must Teach the People

Church leaders will not succeed in breaking down the entrenched attitudes of their congregations overnight. It will require painstaking, persistent teaching. Teaching about the calling of all Christians to be witnesses to their friends about Jesus. Teaching about the need of people for the Savior. Teaching about the privilege of being his ambassadors. Teaching about the importance of relationships, so that church people do not form a ghetto but are out in society acting like yeast or salt. This will, in turn, prove costly to the church. It will be hard for ministers to encourage it, because it will mean that some of the most gifted of their congregations will see their calling more in the boardroom or the union, more in the sports club or the community center, than in internally related church activities. But you can only evangelize friends. And friendships need to be built up and cultivated. It is for lack of them that so many earnest Christian invitations to Christian events fall on deaf ears.

Part of the teaching role of the pastor will be to make a clear distinction between the calling of all Christians to be witnesses and the gifting of some to be evangelists. We all have a story to tell: the story of God's dealings with us, and how he became real to us in the first instance. We ought all to be able to give an account of the hope that is in us, so Peter tells us (1 Pet 3:15). And that is an extremely important function. We may not be able to argue the truth of the faith. We may not be very sure of its content. But if we can say with simple confidence, "Jesus Christ is alive, and I know him," that has an enormous power. For, while your arguments may be rebutted, nobody can deny your experience. And if you are willing humbly to share it when opportunity offers, it will often challenge, intrigue, irritate until your friend decides he or she must look into the matter more closely. And that is when he or she is most in danger from the heavenly Fisherman!

But though all are called to give their story, not all are equipped by God to be evangelists. The talent to explain the way to faith convincingly and clearly, the talent to precipitate decision for Christ, is one of the gifts of the ascended Christ, and it is not given to everyone. But it is given to some. The statisticians reckon that something like one in fourteen of a congregation has the gift of an evangelist. Of course, they may have no idea that they have such a gift. It is your job, if you are the leader in the church, to teach the existence of such gifts (Eph 4:11 puts the matter very plainly) and to look out for those who may be gifted in this way without knowing it. Usually it will become fairly obvious, given encouragement from yourself.

The budding evangelist will often be bringing people to church. He or she will feel very much at home in the company of non-Christians and not in the least embarrassed about being known as a believer—laughing off the jeers and cheerfully accepting the taunts while remaining friends with the mockers! There is your natural evangelist. Generally it is someone who really likes people and is never happier than when in their company. But God is never dull and monolithic. No single personality type can be labeled evangelistic. Some Christians live quiet lives, but there is something about them which prompts others to ask them questions, to which they can respond effectively. Sometimes people do ask, "What is it you've got which I haven't?" or "How can you be so cheerful on a Monday morning?" or, as once happened to me, the dentist's assistant might just say, "How is it that you seem to be happy all the time, even when you get out from the dentist's chair?" Opportunities like this come occasionally to most of us. Frequently we fail to make anything of them. But they come most often to a person whose life exudes an aroma of Christ, and such a person can draw others to the Lord with a minimum of explanation and argument. He or she acts as a sort of conductor for the electricity of God. It gets through. And the friend is drawn to the source of that power, Jesus Christ himself.

They Must Give the Training

It is one thing to begin to discover in the congregation a number of people who might have the gifts of an evangelist. It is quite another to set them on their way. For this they need training. And they will rightly expect the professional pastor to provide it.

There are various ways in which this can be done. The pastor can announce that he is going to offer a course on how one individual can help another to begin a friendship with Jesus Christ. The pastor can either make up his own course, or derive one from books and experience. There is much wisdom in Leighton Ford's *Good News Is for Sharing* (Elgin, Ill.: D.C. Cook, 1977). *Evangelism Explosion* by James Kennedy (Wheaton, Ill.: Tyndale, 1977) is a well-tried method, particularly effective in the United States. *How to Give Away Your Faith* by Paul Little (Downers Grove, Ill.: InterVarsity Press, 1988) is excellent. Others would advocate Bill Bright's *Witnessing Without Fear* (San Bernadino, Calif.: Here's Life Publishers, 1987) or Robert Coleman's *The Master Plan of Evangelism* (Westwood, N.J.: Fleming H. Revell, 1964). It is a great mistake to adopt any of these without making sure that it is suitable for the situation in which you find yourself. I find it better to create a course myself which is geared to members of our church and to their understanding and background. Subjects handled include the mindset of modern people who are indifferent to God; the need of people for the gospel; the person of Jesus and what he has done for mankind through his incarnation, death and resurrection; the way to personal encounter with Christ through repentance, faith and, when appropriate, baptism; the common objections that are met with; the grounds for Christian assurance; and the first steps in Christian growth. Part of the program should be a deliberate attempt by each member to lead one of his or her friends to Christ during the course of the weeks immediately following.

Another much more devastating way of going about it, which may be suitable for brave spirits, especially among young people, is to give people a minimum of verbal training but apprentice them by going out on the streets. You can go out in pairs, armed with a questionnaire, and ask passers-by if you might ask them a few questions. One might be, "Are you a regular worshiper at any church?" This might lead to, "Who do you believe Jesus Christ to have been?" which in turn could give way to some such question as, "If it were possible to meet him, would you want to?" Questions like these, if asked with due sensitivity, can start up really good conversations with complete strangers right on the street. The whole experience is a baptism of fire for the couples as they go out, but they learn no end from it. This also shows that Christians care enough to get out of their buildings and out on the streets. The couples then retire to the church, pray, share experiences and learn from their mistakes.

A third way of training is to make use of a video. There are one or two videos specially designed to help people in sharing their faith. The video, only part of a weekly session, is complemented by role play, discussion and practical experience. An excellent training video called *Person to Person* has been produced in the United Kingdom by the somewhat unlikely coalition of Scripture Union, Campus Crusade and the Bible Society. This widely acclaimed video has won a national award.[1]

But perhaps the best way of training is by apprenticeship. On a number of occasions, someone has brought a friend to me who was on the point of commitment to Christ and asked me to take that friend further. I have done so in the company of both people—the friend and my "apprentice." In this way a person can participate when their friend makes a commitment, and they can get a practical demonstration of how to help another enquirer over that last hurdle or two into faith.

They Must Model the Role
It is a fairly basic principle of leadership that you cannot lead anyone further than you yourself have gotten. Evangelism does not happen in a great many churches for the simple reason that the pastor does

not stress it and, worse still, he or she is not seen doing it. If you are expecting to see a congregation come alive in sharing the good news, then it stands to reason that the leader must be deeply committed to it. One does not need to be very good at it. But one does need to have a go at it. And before long others will emerge whom God has gifted more richly in evangelism.

I think of a mission I had the privilege of leading with a team of Oxford students in Britain. It was a citywide campaign for two weeks in the northern town of Huddersfield. Near the heart of the town there was a marvelous open-air space designed rather like a theater where events could take place and onlookers sit or stand on the steps, with shops and shoppers behind them. We did open-air ministry at lunchtime there each day, using poetry and song, drama and move-ment, testimony and preaching. It usually fell to me to draw things to a conclusion, and we had the joy of seeing a trickle of people coming to Christian commitment as they sat on the steps, talking and then praying with one of our team.

One day I could not take part: I had to speak to the town councilors. So I asked one of the drama team, a senior Oxford student who had been there every day, to close the meeting with a challenge. When I got back I found the students buzzing with the fact that half a dozen people had committed their lives to Christ as a result of my friend's final challenge. I told him that he was much better at it than I and that he would be doing it for the rest of the campaign. God had given him greater gifts than I had for such ministry: But he would never have realized it had not I, as the leader of the church, been prepared to lead the way and then to step aside as a more gifted person emerged. That is the task of modeling.

It is the same with evangelistic preaching in church. Leaders must be prepared to do it, even if they are not particularly talented at it. They must, like Timothy in the New Testament, "do the work of an evangelist" (2 Tim 4:5), even though they are not Paul. They must also be prepared for others to do it instead of them. And it takes a good deal of courage and humility for a pastor to do those two things. Courage, because once you start preaching for decision in church, noses get put out of joint (and they might be the noses of the well-heeled!). And humility, because for the pastor to stand aside and let a layman who is a talented evangelist loose in the congregation is, to say the least, unusual. But it is unquestionably the way to grow evangelists in your church, evangelists who will be able to affect the neighborhood.

They Must Share the Task

From modeling we have already strayed into sharing. It is hard to keep the two apart. For once you begin to practice what you preach, people in the congregation will take note, and those with the love for evangelism will gather round you and want to be involved. It proved to be just like that when I was asked to lead a three-day mission outreach at a nearby university. I agreed to do so and took thirty or so of my class from Regent College with me. We operated in the great hall of the university, in the square, around which much of it was built, in the dormitories, at lunchtime and evening meetings, and at a late-night cabaret-style function. The result was that all our team shared in the ministry, and helped to reap the considerable fruit. All returned back to the college on fire for God and thrilled to have seen him so clearly at work in changing lives. And students who had never seen themselves as evangelists began to discover that God had indeed given them that gift.

I think of a congregation I helped to found in Vancouver. A church was there already, but its congregation was very formal, very old and very small. Attempts to get others to come in and stay in such a worshiping community were conspicuously unsuccessful. We decided to start a new congregation at nine o'clock in the morning, and a small team of us went visiting in the community for that purpose. I had the privilege of preaching evangelistically for five successive weeks to the heterogeneous collection of people who, marvelous to relate, turned up at that unearthly hour on a Sunday morning. But it was a shared enterprise. Some of us visited and brought people to the service. Some shared an extensive time of prayer beforehand. Some provided a small orchestra and visuals for the overhead projector. Some gave testimony to what Christ had done in their lives. And some talked personally to people who wanted to make Christ their own Lord. It was a shared enterprise, and it has grown now into a viable and lively congregation.

So important do I believe this principle of sharing that I rarely accept invitations on my own these days. I try to take a team with me, large or small. It may be over 100 or it may be two or three. The principle is the same in either case—once reconciled with God we are reconciled into a body. And in evangelism we need not only to *proclaim* that reconciliation, but to *exhibit* it by partnership and the quality of our mutual relationships in the team. In this way the unspoken message that comes across from the team reinforces the thrust of the words they speak. And each member of the team grows from being part of a shared enterprise like this.

I think I discovered its importance very early in my ministry. When, as a new pastor in my first job, I began to be asked out to speak at surrounding youth groups, I used to take a few of our own youth group with me. We would pray about the engagement first, and plan what part each would take in it. I found myself less and less of a solo performer, and more and more of a ringmaster, orchestrating the contributions of others in the team. I think we may have done some good where we went. We certainly found the team growing by leaps and bounds. Our Lord did not select solo performers: He chose a team of twelve disciples. We would be wise to emulate his example. In that way we have every reason to hope that the church as a living body will indeed be a continuing evangelistic agency in the neighborhood with a natural and unself-conscious enthusiasm.

They Must Provide the Occasion

As the church becomes more at ease in the realm of evangelism, opportunities will grow. The pastors will be asked elsewhere to speak about the subject or to conduct some mission or outreach. And what they need to do is not to run themselves ragged by responding positively to every invitation, but provide occasion for others in their congregation to go instead. There is a delicate moment when, if you try to do this, you fear it won't work. You reply that you cannot go, but that you would like to recommend So-and-So. They do not take up your suggestion! But persevere. After awhile you *will* be trusted when you say, "Don't take me. Take my friend." Somebody will. And you will be over the hurdle.

I can recall in a previous parish a delightful, cautious, gentle doctor. He was a very good doctor, and he was very dubious indeed about evangelism. I managed to persuade him to come on some team I was taking out. He came, and came again, and again. Now he not only takes teams all over the country as opportunity offers and as his time allows, but he organizes the whole outreach ministry of that church. I drew him in, provided the occasion for him to lead, and now he provides the occasion for taking others. And so the good infection grows.

You do not have to wait for invitations to come in. Once some of your own congregation have got the bit between their teeth, why not suggest the visit of your team to a nearby church? I always feel this is a "no-lose" situation. If your team does well, they return home thrilled, and the receiving congregation is glad to have had some down-to-earth laymen ministering to them instead of the usual pastor! They may well be spurred to do something similar themselves. If your team is a bit shaky and hesitant and does not do well, the same result is usually achieved. The receiving congregation may say, "Huh, we could have done better than that," and they take an opportunity to go and improve on what they have seen! I think of a mission I led with a team from a previous church into one of the large residential country villages in southern England. It so happened, in the providence of God, that this church was poised on the edge of renewal. We happened to come at just the right time. The result was a marvelous weekend in which many people came to Christ, and folk from our own team who had never had the joy of introducing anyone to Jesus discovered it then. The next weekend people who had come to faith crowded up into the pulpit of the receiving congregation to bear testimony to what God had done in their lives. And before long that village was itself sending out teams of enthusiastic, amateur witnesses into the surrounding countryside.

They Must Furnish the Encouragement

Evangelism can be demanding and exhausting. Those who engage in it can easily become burnt-out. Some of the most active evangelists these days are workers with parachurch movements, and I honor

them for their courage and initiative. Yet I have to say that at Regent
College, where I work, we have a steady stream of burnt-out workers
who have left rather battered by their organization. They have been
expected to do primary evangelization by visiting strangers for eight
hours a day and have not received a great deal of encouragement. The
result is that evangelism is emphatically not something they want to
hear about. We all need encouragement, and never more than when
we are engaged in the difficult task of seeking lovingly to change the
whole direction of a life, to bring it back to its proper source and goal
in God.

That is why those who are most engaged in evangelism in the
neighborhood should be especially well cared for: with acts of thought-
fulness, the occasional gift, or a "fun" happening where all they are
expected to do is to relax and enjoy it. If this loving care is exercised,
the budding gifts of young evangelists will have the chance to develop
without being frozen off in the sharp frost of overuse. If it is not, you
will soon be looking for a fresh young evangelist.

You can encourage young evangelists in two or three other obvious
ways. In England there are annual get-togethers of those engaged in
extensive evangelism. To attend a meeting like this among like-
minded peers could be a tremendous encouragement. In North America there are other means of gaining input. Conferences by men like
Billy Graham and members of his team, Leighton Ford, John
Wimber and others, are an occasional treat and an opportunity to be
refreshed, to gain fresh ideas, and to meet with like-minded people.
Another extremely encouraging thing is to be allowed to share in the
nurture of new believers. I am strongly convinced of the value of
discovery groups, or whatever you care to call them. These are short
courses of, say, eight weeks, expressly designed for new converts and
those on the edge of commitment. Leading a discovery group is one
of the joys of my life. And I never count it a greater privilege than
when I have been the human instrument through whom some of the
members came to faith. If you want to stretch and, at the same time,
greatly encourage a young evangelist, put him in a small team leading
a discovery group.

This is not the place to enlarge on the contents of such a group;

suffice it to say that the new believer has particularly pressing needs which cry out for attention. Without that attention and tender loving care, the evangelistic outreach of the church into the neighborhood will grind to a halt. There will be a good many professions of conversion, maybe, but few people will be added to the church and become real disciples. It is vital for all who engage in evangelism to realize that Jesus is interested in disciples, not decisions. And the best initial steps that I know toward building that tentative commitment into sturdy discipleship are discovered in a small group for new Christians. The new believer needs to be clear on the step he or she has taken, the grounds for Christian assurance, the means of growing in the spiritual life, the role of the church and of the Holy Spirit, how to handle temptation, and what Christian service involves. They need to find out about fellowship as they encounter it in one another in the group. They need to learn to pray and to pick verses from Scripture to feed on. It is nothing less than a whole new life for them, and they need all the help they can get. It is an enormous privilege as an evangelist to be allowed from time to time to engage in the leadership of such a group. The growth that happens in those first two months is often staggering, and if anything is calculated to put a fresh spring into the step of a young evangelist, it is this.

They Must Exude the Faith

What is the main difference between a new swimmer and an experienced one? Or between a fledgling bird learning to fly and the parent bird? It is simply confidence. And confidence makes all the difference in evangelism. When I began I was so amazed that God should use human beings in partnership with himself to kindle new life in others, that I was sometimes tentative in laying the issues on the line. I think I was terrified that if I was too clear and decisive nobody would respond, and I might look like a fool or a failure. I guess I am not alone in that unworthy sentiment! What is more, Western culture is so pluralistic that we shy from making absolute claims for Jesus. On the surface at least, our culture is so polite that we feel almost discourteous about putting the knife in and challenging people to repent and believe. Yet that is what Jesus did. He called people to leave their old

way of life, then and there, and to follow him. What is more, he called
them to do it openly. If we are faithful to him, we will do the same.
And with experience, we will find that God honors this holy, loving
boldness.

There ought to be nothing raucous or condemnatory about our challenge and appeal. We should simply put the alternatives on the line
and challenge people in the name of Jesus to make the decision they
know they ought to—when they are ready, and not before. We will
often see fruit, fruit that sometimes amazes us. And when we do not,
we will learn, like the farmer, to wait for the good seed to germinate,
confident in the God of nature and the God of grace that it will. His
Word will not return to him void. It never does. And the older I get
the more often I see instances of people who heard the good news
from me and who had come to faith even though I never knew it.

This evangelism is God's work. God is the evangelist. It is his Word
that creates new life once sown in the soil of human hearts. It is his
Spirit who convicts of sin, makes Jesus glorious in the eye of the
enquirer, and brings him to new birth and assurance that God is his
Abba, Father. None of us can do it. But in evangelism we are priv-
ileged to cooperate with God. We must make sure that we do so on
his terms. It is his peace initiative which we hold out to rebel hearts.
We have no right to change those conditions of repentance, faith,
commitment and baptism into the body of Christ which he laid down.
And curiously enough, most people prefer such a challenge to some
milk-and-water message which they know in their bones is short-
selling them. If neighborhood evangelism is to take off, it will never
do so on some half-baked gospel. Only the authentic bread of New
Testament Christianity will feed hungry stomachs, and we must have
no truck with a pusillanimous approach.

It has struck me, as a newcomer to North America, that we need
to get back to the plain, commonsense directness of Jesus and the
apostles. There is a tendency in American circles to rant and rave
about the gospel. That is not required of us. There is a tendency in
Canada to walk around the gospel like an Indian in moccasins, terrified of putting anyone off or suggesting that one way is better than
another! Let us go for the happy mean, the biblical mean, of a con-

fident, warm, direct presentation of the good news. We have nothing to be embarrassed about. The Lord has visited his people, estranged though we were by our innate self-centeredness. He has come in person. He has dealt with the human predicament at its tap root, by absorbing our guilt and wickedness into his own person on that terrible cross. He was victorious in that ultimate battle. The grave could not hold him. He is alive. He can be met. And we have met him and want to share that relationship with others. How can anyone be ashamed of such outstanding good news? How can anyone water it down until it fits in with the ever-changing climate of the age? We have every reason for confidence in the gospel.

When that confidence is deeply rooted in our soul several things happen. As we preach we have a note of authority (not authoritarianism), the authority of truth. As we preach, young evangelists are encouraged by the power of the Word of God and the impact it makes on the attention and lives of the hearers. As we preach, men and women begin their journey back to God. And what greater privilege could we have than that? One of our great needs today is an army of men and women who have such confidence in Christ and his good news that they exude that faith as they speak and live their daily lives. Then we shall see a whole new generation of younger evangelists cropping up in church after church, who will make a significant influence on their neighborhoods for God.

Seven

Skilled Marriage Builders

With one in three marriages ending in divorce, every church leader in North America knows that building strong marriages is crucial. But the question is how? No program seems sufficient for the task. The reason is that healthy marriages are encouraged more by healthy families and healthy churches than by short programs and seminars. The quality of the church's corporate life will prove to be a fundamental equipping factor for married Christians *when they are not in church meetings.* We need a systemic rather than a programmatic approach. But this approach seems to make marriage ministry even more overwhelming to the thoughtful church leader.

The average pastor today feels like a general medical practitioner in a small isolated city, a city high in the mountains, largely cut off from the outside world of resources, having no hospital and no specialist doctors in the area. As the only resource person, he is confronted with too many needs and very complicated diseases.

Think of the various dimensions of marriage ministry urgently needed in the church today:

☐ premarital preparation of never-married couples

☐ sex education dealing with premarital sexuality among young adults

☐ training in appropriate Christian dating patterns

☐ marriage-enrichment ministries

☐ marriage therapy in groups and through personal counseling

☐ intervention in abusing spouses and marital crises

☐ conciliation and/or reconciliation ministry

☐ divorce recovery and support ministries for divorcing persons

☐ premarital counseling of remarrying couples

☐ marital healing dealing with sexual hurts and painful memories

☐ spiritual friendship-building between spouses

In the smaller church with one staff person, trying to develop a marriage ministry could be depressing unless one is absolutely convinced that the pastor is not the minister of the church. Jesus is the minister, and he chooses to minister through the whole church, not just the pastor. Marriage ministry is no exception to this.

Meet the Marriage Minister

My conviction is that all the roles in marriage ministry are church roles, not just pastor roles. Look at them:

☐ *teacher* of biblical marriage patterns

☐ *model-maker,* providing multiple models for marrying couples

☐ *networker,* developing significant and supportive relationships

☐ *counselor*

☐ *celebrant* of the marriage vows

☐ *healer* of family and marriage wounds

☐ *enricher* and renewer of the marriage covenant

These are too complex and varied to be embodied in one superstar pastor. They were meant to be shared by the body. The task of pastors and leaders in local churches, is not to *do* all of this ministry, but to equip the saints for the work of the ministry (Eph 4:11-12). Strategically, this means equipping the *church* so that the church equips the saints. Equipping the individual member without equipping the whole church is a half-measure.

Discerning the Body

I feel justified in pursuing a medical/organic analogy of equipping for good reasons. To speak of the church as a body is no mere metaphor hinted at in the Gospels (Jn 2:21) and expounded by Paul (for example, Eph 1:22-23; 2:16; 3:6; 4:4, 12, 16; 5:23, 28-30). It is literally true that if one member of the body hurts, all suffer (1 Cor 12:26). It is not only unloving but untrue for one member of the body to say to another, "I don't need you!" (1 Cor 12:21). The basic unit of the church according to Paul is not the individual member but the church in its bodily life. Therefore, Paul says, "In Christ we who are many form one body, and each member belongs to all the others" (Rom 12:5). The medical-body analogy has a further endorsement in the root meaning of the word for equipping. The classical usage of the Greek word for equipping *(katartizō)* describes what a doctor does when he "equips" a body that has a broken bone or a dislocated member. He puts it back into correct relationship with the other members of the body. Equipping, like the work of the doctor, is corrective and creative, but always relational.

One reason why we are not equipped to nurture marriages is that we do not look at the way the body is put together—how it works and functions. The approach based on a lay training kit with videos and student manuals will be as satisfying as cold mashed potatoes once one sees the body with equipping eyes. What I am probing as an alternative is a systems model derived by medical analogy.

To equip systemically one must not merely look at the body but *into* it. A doctor must do that, and so must an equipper. The equipper with "equipping eyes" does not merely see the hand and foot; he sees its structure, its genetic make-up, its living connections.

Four Equipping Systems

To ease our way into "systems" thinking I want to explore four subsystems of the human body as analogies for equipping the church for marriage ministry. The first system is all-important, since it makes all the vital connections in the body.

The Nervous System:

The Equipper as a Neurologist

■ Connections with the Head

■ Relationships between Members

■ Gift-Ministry at the Point of Connection ("Joints")

The Nervous System: The Equipper As a Neurologist

Nerves are sensors and circuits for carrying messages from one part of the body to another. The nervous system is a maze of connections. Nerve cells carrying electrical signals have at the point of their connection (synapses) a forest of branches touching and joining other cells. Signals jump from cell to cell with the help of chemical messengers. The brain, the "head" of the system, is directly responsible for the control and articulation of the whole body. Without the brain we could not function in an integrated way. A neurologist tries to find out why some messages are blocked and others are so intense that the body is in pain. The physician will be especially concerned if one part of the body is paralyzed.

Equipping facilitates the connection of the head of the church, Jesus, to every member. Relationships are the primary expression of this connection, and gifts are the various kinds of connections in the body. Gift ministry is not something an individual does, one's "thing." It is the ministry of Jesus at the point of connection in the body— "joined and held together by every supporting ligament" (Eph 4:16) or "by every joint" (4:16 RSV).

Gifts are expressions of a relational ministry. Without relationships gifts are unthinkable. What we give to one another in body-life are not mere messages "but our lives as well" (1 Thess 2:8). Sensation, coordination and articulation cannot be restored to a body unless the right connections are made. The neurologist knows this; so does the equipper. We need all our nerves as we need every member and every charism, or grace, given by God through his people. "The eye cannot say to the hand, 'I don't need you' " (1 Cor 12:21). God has placed each member in an interdependent connection "just as he determines" (12:11). He has determined; we must discern what he has determined in order to equip the body for ministry. Now I will relate this to equipping the church to nurture healthy marriages.

We should think of the church as an iceberg, nine-tenths hidden underwater (the real systemic life) and one-tenth (the formal seminars and training programs we may offer) above water. Relationships are part of the hidden but persuasive message about covenant-making and covenant-keeping in marriage. This is especially true if the church is characterized by *kinship,* if it is familial rather than institutional. We are brothers and sisters, parents, children, aunts and uncles, not replaceable but functioning parts in an organization. Let me explain more exactly how these relational "nerves" can affect marriage ministry.

☐ *Prizing every member for who they are evokes covenant interdependence.* For four years my father, a stroke victim, lay in the hospital unable to speak, eat or move. In his prime years he had been an aggressive and active man, moving from driving the "Stevens Bread and Cake" van for his father to becoming president of a steel fabrication company.

In the evenings he worked in the garden or built things. But after the stroke he could not *do* anything; he just was, but he was very precious. He has now passed into a heavenly environment in which everyone prizes him for being himself rather than for what he did or didn't do in this life. Every time I visited him in the hospital, and I never found those visits easy, I confronted a searching question. Am I valuable to myself and to others not because of anything I do or can produce but simply because I *belong* to someone?

Children don't *do* anything for us. Just the reverse: We must do almost everything for them, at least in earliest infancy. But they *do* the one thing needful for us; they remind us that we are precious just because we belong. Perhaps Jesus had this in mind when he said we must become like little children. Many of us will get a chance to do it when we are old. But we can evoke something crucial to marriage health by prizing people for who they are in the local church, not merely for what they do to serve the church.

□ *Parity in male-female ministries in the church models interdependence in marriage.* A church that formalizes women's roles as "serving sandwiches and giving child care," and men's roles as "decision-making and influencing" is modeling a role description incongruous with Ephesians 5:21-33 where the husband is called to be the server and care-giver to his wife. How can we hope to build companionship marriages when local churches orchestrate hierarchies in which women are under men?

□ *Doing for one another what we can as a church family nurtures covenant relationships rather than contractual obligations.* In Robert Frost's "The Death of the Hired Hand," a farmer defines family this way: "Home is the place where, when you have to go there, they have to take you in." But the farmer's wife responded with a better definition: "I should have called it something you somehow haven't to deserve."[1] There is something like an unlimited liability for one another, an economic community of sharing in both church and biblical marriage.

That was certainly the case with the Jerusalem church where "there were no needy persons among them" (Acts 4:34). Someone called this a "religious communism of love." It is a good description of marriage. Biblical marriage is an unconditional covenant of belonging, not a conditional contract for mutual obligations. A church experience that is "for better, for worse" is a formative environment for healthy marriages. Such sharing of life and resources, both personal and material, requires family stability, which is difficult for the average North American, who moves every four years. Should we not challenge people to give their marriage and family some stability by remaining in the fellowship of one church for a decade or more, "for better, for worse"?

□ *Intergenerational learning in the church is a relational resource for marriages.* Every local church has a great untapped resource in the persons of couples who have a mature marital covenant. That is why I encourage the home model of premarital counseling: A mature lay couple counsels a couple preparing for marriage. We should encourage young couples to interview several marital pioneers before getting married themselves. Generally, I believe the pastor should not do premarital counseling because the church (and mature couples in it) can do it better!

These four examples of how the nervous system works in the body underline the truth that the church is not a "happening" but a beautiful, integrated and articulated organism, exactly the context needed for growing in covenant.

Marriage is not a contract for rendering mutual services, but a covenant for mutual belonging, "for better, for worse . . . until death do us part." A local church that lives as the new covenant community and evokes covenant relationships rather than short-term contractual relationships, will nurture healthy marriages. But let us take another system in the body.

The Digestive System:

The Equipper as a Nutritionist

- Teaching

- Bible Learning

- Life-Centered Experiential Learning

- Theological Reflection on Ministry

The Digestive System: The Equipper As a Nutritionist
Without food the body cannot live. We do not live to eat, but we must eat to live. The nutritionist makes sure we have a well-balanced diet.

The digestive system extracts nutrients from the environment to maintain homeostasis, that marvelous balance toward which the body constantly strives in face of constant change. The stomach and intestines absorb nutrients through a wall that manifests folding, infolding and microfolding like the pile of a towel. This part of the body is built for absorption. The problem with the church body is that some people live to eat. They never get beyond taking in unapplied biblical data. They suffer from informational overload, never getting beyond cognitive learning, which, biblically speaking, is not knowledge at all. As Francis of Assisi said, "Mankind has as much knowledge as it executes."

Here are some concrete plans that offer nurture *with response.*

☐ *The marriage-enrichment weekend* is one of the most useful resources that a church can offer its couples. It has been said that David and Vera Mace think they know more than anyone else about this, and they probably do. The Maces say that "the goal in a marriage-enrichment event is to create an environmental setting that will enable a couple to receive significant new information, process it as knowledge, use it to gain deeper insight into their interpersonal relationship, trying this out in terms of new ways of interacting with each other, and together make a commitment to achieve further relational growth through the necessary behavioral changes."[2]

In my experience this works best in a fairly romantic setting, like a hotel or retreat center with private rooms, away from family and work responsibilities. Pastors officiating at weddings should require this of couples during their first year. It is not a remedy for very needy marriages.

But significant change can begin for those whose marriages have become routinized. We have seen some people yield their lives to Christ for new life and others renew their vows. On a memorable weekend one couple went out to the rocky point at our favorite seaside lodge for such weekends and for the first time said their vows to each other. They had been married at the registry office two years before and went home from the weekend saying they had *really* got married and were married for good.

☐ *Second-level weekends* are an effective way of equipping couples to get involved in marriage ministry. Having come to a "general" weekend, they can learn in a more intensive growth and communication experience. Then leaders of the marriage ministry may select "presenting couples" from these more skilled people to share their experiences in future general weekends.

☐ A *"couples' journey" or "good companions" event* can be planned in which experienced couples or a resource person in the church addresses a marriage theme each month. This makes a good neighborhood outreach.

☐ A *marriage-enrichment elective* in the adult Sunday school or adult education offerings puts the marriage ministry into the mainstream of Christian education. My two books on marriage, *Married for Good* and *Marriage Spirituality* have exercises and study questions at the end of each chapter which can be used in groups or classes.

☐ *Marriage-related Bible study guides* can be used in small groups meeting in homes. My wife, Gail, and I have published one with Harold Shaw Publishers: *Marriage: Learning from Couples in Scripture.*

☐ A *series on marriage* can be given in Sunday sermons.

☐ An *integrated curriculum on family* that includes both marriage and singleness can be written for congregational use. As we discovered in chapter one, each week the integrated curriculum has a passage of Scripture to be studied alone, as a small group and through the public proclamation, providing a cumulative impact.

☐ *Good books on marriage* can be placed in the church library. Check the bibliography for a list of possible resources.

Each of these strategies may have a multiple impact in the context of a local church's life, especially where they are not merely programs inserted from the outside. Like the human body, the local church is self-regulating. No local church can tolerate a steady diet of marriage teaching. It will be most effective when it is one of many nurturing strategies.

But educational nurture is only part of marriage ministry, usually the *only* part we think about. The next system calls the pastor to be an environmental engineer, or a hematologist.

The Circulatory System:

The Equipper as a Hematologist

- Symbols and Cues

- The Environmental Factors

- People-Prizing

_ Experimental

- Worshipful

- Expectant

- Love

The Circulatory System: The Equipper As a Hematologist

"The life . . . is in the blood" (Lev 17:11) is not only a profound theological statement about the inner logic of sacrifice for sin. It is also a bodily truth. Blood affects everything—energy level, ability to fight infection, regulation of temperature and excretion. It is the environment of life as a million red and white corpuscles in serum course through the miles of conduits in the human body from the heart and lungs to the extremities. The blood bathes every cell in the body with a solution that contains everything needed. Receptors in each organ, like locks that fit particular keys, take from the blood what that organ requires: energy in the form of sugar, minerals, hormonal messages and antibodies. Blood links everything. It is the body's atmosphere.

Perhaps the most significant aspect in equipping theology and methodology is this matter of atmosphere or environment. Kenneth Van Wyk wrote his doctoral dissertation on the factors that affect the full release of lay ministry. Through extensive surveys, he uncovered what is seldom appreciated: Most churches concentrate on equipping by offering courses that focus on content but fail to release significant lay ministry until they consider the environmental factor. Van Wyk writes:

Every congregation has an attitudinal climate. This "feeling" is a powerful determiner of how adequately the ministry of Christ is carried out by lay people. A sense of enthusiasm gets people unstuck. A passionate nucleus of committed tent-making ministers can energize and motivate the whole body. Dullness, on the other hand, curtails involvement.[3]

A number of important factors determine the learning environment, including verbal and nonverbal clues and symbols that tell a person whether their movement into ministry will be worthwhile. Communication experts tell us that ninety-three per cent of communication is nonverbal! Actual words account for only seven per cent; tone of voice and everything else is the environment which really does the talking. We can communicate the right message if we are sensitive to environmental factors. Here are some concrete examples of environmental engineering.

☐ *Introduce couples together, and have couples minister together where possible.* This symbolizes commitment to the marital subsystem. In no way, however, should we communicate to singles that they have less status, especially since in most urban churches today half the members are singles. Couples and singles are kin.

☐ *When only one partner is asked to accept some responsibility, we prize marriage when we consult both partners together.* We need to explore carefully what effect one spouse's becoming an elder or a Sunday-school superintendent would have on the other. This is more than relational courtesy; it is a statement about the body system. As I mentioned before, if one member of a body is moved, all the other members must compensate. For example, when a homemaker becomes a church elder substantial change is required on the part of the spouse. So both should be consulted.

☐ *Publicly it is important to urge people not to come to everything offered in the church* and always to make sure they have time to relax on the sofa with their spouse or to hang over the back fence and talk to a neighbor.

☐ *Recognize engagements, weddings and anniversaries in the life of the community.* This allows us to minister to couples at significant marker events in their lives. Some churches have an opportunity every Sunday for people to come forward for prayers on their birthdays or anniversaries or if they have a special need for healing prayer. That domesticates marriage ministry.

But where would all this be without structure? The body would be an amorphous blob!

The Bone-Muscle System:

The Equipper as an Orthopedist

■ Patterns of Body Life

■ Appropriately
   Sized
   Located
   Timed
   Situated

■ Flexible and Discardable

The Bone-Muscle System: The Equipper As an Orthopedist

Bones give structure to the body. Muscles give movement. Together they contribute form and freedom. What is so amazing about the way we are fearfully and wonderfully made is how parts of our body, like bones, are constantly being renewed.

Almost one-third of the body's blood is in the bones, and the bones themselves are continually being dissolved and reformed. Every atom of our body is replaced every few years, including the bones. Some church committees are eternal, but our bones get replaced every two years. Our form looks the same, but we are always in flux even in our structural members. That is the case in a living organism but not in a lifeless organization.

When a bone is broken or out of joint the whole body suffers. As indicated above, *katartizō*, medically speaking, means setting the bones straight. Equipping is a structural ministry, a wineskin ministry. New wine calls for new wineskins (Mt 9:17), appropriate vessels to contain the living ferment that is life in Christ.

By using this image, Jesus suggests that the church is a kind of brewery, full of so much fermentation and experimentation that we must always be looking for new ways to contain and channel renewal. If we fail to find appropriate structures or adhere to old ones, Jesus warns that the new life will be wasted and the old containers will get destroyed.

Small groups are the single most significant structure for equipping the saints and taking marriage ministry home—literally. Small groups with a mission focus or a special interest, can maximize the resources of the body. David and Vera Mace suggest several proposals for small groups committed to marriage ministry[4]:

☐ *A marriage support group* of four or five couples may meet for follow-up after a marriage-enrichment weekend. If a couple makes a commitment during the weekend to meet for eight weeks, they have a greater probability of getting the kind of support they need to accomplish the behavioral changes they want.

☐ *Growth groups* could provide a six- to eight-week intensive exposure to one selected area of marital enrichment, such as conflict resolution, gender roles or sexual communication.

☐ *Couple evangelism* may be one of the most neglected but most fruitful forms of evangelism. At a Marriage Helper Training Seminar, Gerry and Pam heard a local Christian psychologist, Paddy Ducklow, remark that most couples come to him for counseling five years too late.

"That settles it," Pam said on the way home. "We're going to get to them five years sooner!" So they bought a study guide from a Christian bookstore and, after praying, went to their neighbors with a winsome invitation: "Gerry and I are going to be doing a marriage-enrichment study ourselves every Thursday evening for the next eight weeks. *We need it,* especially in this day and age. If you want to join us come on over." Several neighbors came and some have not only enriched their marriages but have embraced Christ.

Here are four systemic ways of equipping the church for marriage ministry. Which system is most important? The body-life equipper dare not even think about that. Each system needs the other. Each system needs to be healthy. And the whole is more than the sum of the parts, as Aristotle said so long ago.

Eight

Justice-Workers
in Society

Pastor Marvin has a problem.[1] *One of his pastoral team has* just been arrested by the police—and not for the first time. Co-pastor Jim just finished serving three months in jail for obstructing the entrance to the Everywoman's Health Clinic, a local abortion center. The court had instructed him not to return, but as soon as Jim got out of jail he went back. He is profoundly evangelical and loves to share the gospel with his fellow prisoners, but he also believes that Christians have to put their lives on the line for contemporary social issues. Jim was aware of what Martin Luther once said: "If you preach the Gospel in all respects with the exception of the issues which deal specifically with your time you are not preaching the Gospel at all."[2]

But this leaves Pastor Marvin with a problem. Should he encourage others in his church to join the protest and possibly get arrested too? Should he restrict himself to preaching the gospel without any reference to the social and societal consequences? How can he minister to the many who feel guilty about not doing what Pastor Jim does, even though they agree abortion has become a silent holocaust? And most important, how can he help equip the church for a fully biblical mission that includes social justice? Typically, evangelical Christians focus on personal evils, evils which could have been prevented by the decision of an individual, rather than the larger evils. But we must learn to deal with systemic evil. That is what we will explore now, using the four systems from the last chapter.

The Digestive System—Teaching Christian Mission

The stomach and intestines absorb nutrients through a wall that is like the pile of a towel, rolled, and then infolded again with maximum absorption. The equipping pastor should be concerned with absorption of teaching, not merely the delivery of information. Educational research shows that we learn most when a life situation makes us ask a question. The prolonged crisis in Pastor Marvin's church over his colleague's incarceration was such a teachable moment.

Week by week, people in the local church encounter a bewildering variety of opportunities for mission on their own doorstep: caring for single parents, reaching non-Christian neighbors, confronting the plague of pornography, appealing to city council to assist with housing for the underprivileged, working to stem the rising tide of divorce, and visiting prisoners. Farther afield unreached people groups wait to hear the good news of Jesus, starving millions die of malnutrition and a growing multitude of refugees look for homes and citizenship. But are all these activities *Christian mission?* Are not some merely good works that redeemed people perform and not essential expressions of the coming Kingdom of Jesus? Pastor Marvin had a nutritional task: to teach the people through sermons, adult classes and casual one-to-one conversations, the nature of Christian mission.

Understanding the Church's Mission

Mission is everything that Jesus sent the church into the world to do, according to his words: "As the Father has sent me, I am sending you" (Jn 20:21). Jesus brought a whole gospel for the whole person (Lk 4:18-20). His ministry included *demonstrating* a new kingdom lifestyle (Jn 13:15; 17:21), *proclaiming* good news (Mt 28:20; Mk 16:15), *healing* the sick and delivering those bound by Satan (Mt 9:35; 10:1), *mediating* and integrating people who otherwise could never form a community (Mk 3:13-19), *serving* sacrificially (Mt 20:28; Lk 22:27), and finally *challenging the powers* in his final nonviolent act of self-giving on the cross (Col 2:15). We who live in Christ are his vehicle for continuing his mission on earth. This mission should never be reduced to a privatized religion of personal salvation. Unfortunately, Christians frequently insist on doing this. Further, those who try to deal with root causes are often regarded with suspicion. Archbishop Romero of South America said that if he feeds the poor they call him a saint, but if he asks why the poor are poor they call him a communist. Mission must deal with root causes, not merely individual effects.

Mission is what the people of God do to serve God and the world. In his classic treatment of lay theology, Hendrik Kraemer says that our preoccupation with the metaphor of the body, what he calls "body-obsession," has resulted in focusing on one of the many biblical terms and images of the church. Unfortunately this concentration caters to a self-serving bias in church ministry. The body maintains and builds itself, and nonprofessional ministers, thinking that ministry is body-directed, become "camouflaged ecclesiastics and clericized lay people."[3] The Bible is rich in other images and metaphors to express what and who the laity are: the bride of Christ, the ecclesia, the colony of heaven, the household of faith, the temple of God, the Israel of God, and especially the people of God.

The church does not "have" a mission as one activity among many to which interested (even called) persons might devote themselves. It "is" mission. The church exists on behalf of the world, not on behalf of itself. The "gifts" of the ascended Christ are not to fill the church but to "fill the whole universe" (Eph 4:10). Paul assures us that "the heavenly places" are not "up there" but the spiritual dimensions of the here and now. He maintains that God's "intent was that now, through the church, the manifold wisdom of God should be made known to the rulers and authorities in the heavenly realms, according to his eternal purpose which he accomplished in Christ Jesus our Lord" (Eph 3:10-11). Therefore the laity is the proper missionary body of the church. The form of the church's mission is merely the form of Christ's own mission: incarnation, crucifixion, resurrection and ultimate glorification. As Kraemer says, "If the laity of the Church, dispersed in and through the world, are really what they are called to be, the real interrupted dialogue between the Church and world happens through them. They form the daily repeated projection of the Church into the world. They embody the meeting of the Church and World."[4]

Celebrating the Church's Impressive Record

In contrast to the taunt "that the church has never done the world any good," the record of what God's people have accomplished in that "daily repeated projection" is impressive indeed. Under the pagan Roman Empire, Christians established the first burial societies during plagues. They cared for the shipwrecked and exiles. They cared for slaves as individual persons of value. They provided for the unemployed by finding work. When the empire was "Christianized," Christians took the lead in seeing that abortion was a punishable offense. They prevented the exposure of children, restricted the gladiatorial fights and tempered the law on capital offenses. While they did not abolish slavery they lessened its evils by forming a Christian community in which slaves were equal with their masters. They promoted Sunday observance, cared for prisoners and labored to improve the lot of women.

In later centuries the church was the first to establish hospitals, asylums, orphanages, homes for fallen women, hostelries, and houses for strangers. The Church founded universities and kept alive the intellectual life for centuries when there was no other agency. The emancipation of the slaves, while long in coming, was first associated with the church in the Edict of Constantine and finally accomplished by significant initiatives of Christians. Women were given greater dignity: The idea of being purchased in marriage largely disappeared, and wives attained limited partnership of property with their husbands. Christians redeemed war captives from servitude. When secular schools disappeared in the sixth century, monastic schools replaced them. In the Middle Ages the church "gave the world a new type of social worker in the Friar, a new pattern of outdoor ministry in St. Francis, and a new model of kingship under St. Louis."[5] The Christian faith has been largely responsible for the movement to give women legal status, the vote and social equality. In recent centuries the world mission of the church has spread civilization and pioneered in education.[6]

In *The Social Achievements of the Christian Church,* E. H. Oliver says that the church has the fivefold function as servant: It must exercise its age-long prophetic role of serving as the conscience of society; it must educate and inspire; it must be the pioneer; it must study and seek to prevent rather than cure; it must transform the helped into helpers.[7]

Unpacking the Church's Mission Today

In light of this impressive record and the more influential Word of God, it seemed inconceivable to Pastor Marvin to reduce the mission of the church to something privatized and irrelevant to the issues of the day. He had heard it said that social justice without evangelism is like sowing grains of sand in the earth, but evangelism without social justice quickly heads in the direction of superstition. So like two blades of the scissors, these two aspects of mission needed to be married again. He started teaching the social implications of the gospel to his congregation on the subject of abortion. "At this moment in history," he said, "it is crucial that the church speak and act prophetically and redemptively, neither silently consenting to evil, nor merely condemning wrong-doers."[8]

But knowing that several women in his congregation had experienced abortion firsthand, he preached the personal and eternal implications of the gospel: "Our Christian preaching must address this abortion issue, among others, both by proclaiming the Lord's view of the dignity of human life, but also by proclaiming the good news of the Lord's compassion and forgiveness for those who turn to him in their sin, sorrow and suffering. The Church proclaims and offers forgiveness and healing for those who have had an abortion." But faithful proclamation demanded that Pastor Murray be utterly honest about the sins of the Christian community and the moral ambiguity of the issue. He and his elders composed a pastoral statement to guide the congregation on this complex issue. Part of it included these words:

As Christians we confess our own sinfulness, not only because many of us have either had an abortion, caused one, or encouraged one, but because we have not provided a serious alternative in long-term care and support for a mother with an unwanted pregnancy. Nor have we helped the male inseminator to accept his full loving responsibility for the conception.

While we repudiate abortion on demand, we admit that there may be some instances where a therapeutic abortion may be the most compassionate choice, specifically, when the mother's physical life is endangered. The regulation of these instances is a matter of social responsibility and must not be left to the individual and her doctor. When such procedures are undertaken, the Christian does so, as with similar ambiguous ethical decisions, with repentance and a prayer for forgiveness.

Further, he and his elders affirmed the primacy of caring for persons. The center of the church's mission is the individual person, and the circumference is the totality of life in this world. Therefore they encouraged the believers to increase their care of both mothers and unborn children wherever possible.

But there is more to doing mission than preaching. Evangelism and social justice are like the two ingredients of common salt: sodium and chlorine. Each separately is a dangerous poison, but taken together they are life-giving. The mission of the church must address root causes, including structural and political factors, or it may be merely rescuing individual souls. The environment in which the church engages in mission, whether proclamation, healing, mediation or service, is cosmic. So, our second analogy comes into play: the circulatory system.

The Circulatory System—Spiritual Warfare

In chapter seven we explored the illuminating analogy in the circulation of the blood. It is the environment of the body, and environmental influences prove more potent than mere informational ones. When we last explored environmental issues, we looked at environmental factors *within* the gathered life of the church that could evoke giftedness and ministry. Now we are looking at environment in a larger sense, because the church is an "open" system that interacts with the world, especially since its members are dispersed in society for almost one hundred and sixty-four hours per week. Just as the blood is the environment of the body and determines what defenses and nutrients are supplied to every member and organ, so church engages in mission against the backdrop of a cosmic conflict. The pastor's privilege is to draw back the curtains through biblical exposition and practical application so ordinary Christians can understand why dealing with an issue like abortion or poverty is so complex.

Evading the Conflict

By and large Western culture has eliminated spiritual warfare without being able to account adequately for the difficulty we all encounter. It was Gerald Heard who said: "Newton banished God from nature, Darwin banished Him from life, and now Freud has banished Him from his last stronghold, the soul."[9] Commenting on this, James Stewart insightfully adds that not only the divine has been banished but the demonic. Paul's conflict with forces, powers and persons who have a malignant grip on our souls has been deemed unreasonable since Newton left no room for an irrational principle in nature, no "mystery of iniquity." Darwin's picture of the biological struggle for existence seemingly supersedes the cosmic struggle between the kingdom of God and "the spiritual forces of evil in the heavenly realms" (Eph 6:12). And Freud effectively explained the powers of darkness as psychological complexes and neuroses so that, as James Stewart says, "the good fight of faith becomes simply a matter of inner individual adjustment."[10] But the problem is deeper than individual human sin or what human nature has become through sin (the flesh). Paul says our struggle is *not* against flesh" (Eph 6:12).

Scripture uses a variety of words for these powers: "rulers," "authorities," "the spiritual forces of evil in the heavenly realms," "thrones" (Rom 8:38; 1 Cor 15:24; Eph 1:21; 3:10; 6:12; Col 1:16; 2:10, 15).[11] The layperson encounters these powers as structures, media, ideologies, forces of social conformity, personages, influences and systems that seem impossible to change, that have a life of their own. Sometimes multinational corporations take on such a role and make such demands on us that they appear to have been co-opted by Satan to woo us from a simple love of God and people. Christian service workers in churches or parachurch society encounter the same difficulties with Christian organizations, though in a more subtle form. Churches are hard to change. So it does not matter whether one is lay or clerical, service means dealing with the powers.

God's Good Gift of "the Powers"

Christians seldom acknowledge that these powers are *not* innately evil. Far from being the result of the fall and a necessary restriction of man's fleshly nature to protect man from himself, these powers are part of God's good creation. Paul claims that through Christ "all things were created: things in heaven and on earth, visible and invisible, whether thrones or powers or rulers or authorities; all things were created by him and for him" (Col 1:16). Theologian Hendrikus Berkhof explains it this way, "Creation has a visible foreground, which is bound together with and dependent on an invisible background. The latter comprises the Powers. These as well were created through and unto Christ; that is, God's love, the same which came to us in Christ, is also the ground and goal of the Powers.... From their very creation, by their very nature, they were 'made to measure' to serve as instruments of this love.... They are the dikes with which God encircles His good creation, to keep it in His fellowship and protect it from chaos."[12]

The Colonization of "the Powers"

These good gifts of God (Col 1:16) were intended to form a framework in which we serve God. They have now become broken, hostile, resistant to God's rule, intransigent. Some of these powers have taken on a life of their own, making idolatrous claims on human beings: government, religion, culture, "isms" and the demonic, being symbolized by the names and "titles" (Eph 1:21) that dominate the news. Scripture describes the predicament of the "principalities and powers" in various ways. Sometimes we are told to regard these pretentious, tyrannical powers as "weak and miserable principles," that make godlike claims but which are "not gods" (Gal 4:8-9). In Ephesians, Paul says that our struggle is not against human problems (flesh and blood) but against "the spiritual forces of evil in the heavenly realms," suggesting that the devil has co-opted these powers, or "colonized" them for his own ends (Eph 6:10-13). Human beings cannot possibly function in this world without encountering these habitual, fallen patterns, which are experienced in competition, in compelling forces of conformity, and in direct satanic attack through witchcraft and satanism.

Some Christian authors treat these powers *only* as structures of our worldly life having no relationship with the devil or fallen angels.[13] Other authors concentrate exclusively on the devil as our spiritual enemy and the focus of our spiritual warfare.[14] But Scripture witnesses both to structures and spiritual hosts as agents and arenas of spiritual warfare.

Because the principalities and powers are Christ's creation, they are not demonic in themselves. Rather, they are demonic because they have been co-opted by Satan in the tragic civil war in the universe, which Satan himself incited. My Kenyan friends have a special way of using the word *colonize* for this, because colonization is something they have thrown off, at great cost. They say that education, government, the media, tribalism, customary laws have been *colonized by Satan.* Our spiritual enemy uses God-created structures as a front for his own scheme, which is to win people away from a simple love-relationship with God.

Not only is Satan colonizing, in some situations he rules directly: among the demonized and Satanists. So discernment is the first crucial ministry of the Christian who serves in the world. Take an executive in a large infant formula manufacturing company, for instance. Is it good business, and worthy of a Christian, to participate in a sales campaign for infant feeding formula in Third-World countries where the polluted water to be added will kill many of the in-

fants? And is it worthy of a Christian, at a lower level of responsibility
in the same company, to participate in manufacturing this good product that will be used, to the company's advantage, in situations where
death and disadvantage will ensue? Yet changing a matter like this
turns out to be a complex matter involving international financing,
competitive capitalism, and all the internal politics of a large corporation. It is spiritual warfare. But the church in mission must not lay
down passively before such powers as though we were helpless vic-
tims. Christ came not only to save souls but to bring peace to the
powers.

Peacing "the Powers"

Christ's relation to the powers is especially important for lay theology.
Christ was voluntarily "victimized" by the powers, as symbolized by
the three-language title over his cross: Latin for government, Greek
for culture and Hebrew for religion. Each brought Christ to the cross,
but he triumphed over all three. Ironically, Christ's death put the
principalities and powers in their place as instruments, subject to
God's sovereignty. Christ disarmed the powers, "made a public spectacle of them" (thereby showing how illusionary their pretensions
were), and triumphed over them (Col 2:15). Speaking to this, Berkhof
says, "The weapon from which they heretofore derived their strength
is struck out of their hands. This weapon was the power of illusion,
their ability to convince men that they were the divine regents of the
world, ultimate certainty and ultimate direction, ultimate happiness
and the ultimate duty for small, dependent humanity. Whenever [the
cross] is preached, the unmasking and disarming of the Powers takes
place."[15]

Apart from the eye of faith, these powers still seem almost omnip-
otent. But to the eye of faith they are vanquished, even though they
continue to press their claims and therefore complicate the Christian's
life in this world. The first and most effective strategy against the
false claims of the powers is preaching the gospel. As Berkhof says,
"The Powers are still present; but whenever Christ is preached and
believed in, a limit has been set to their working."[16] Our duty is not
to bring the powers to *our* knees: This is Christ's task. Our duty is

to arm ourselves with Christ (Eph 6:10-18) and to preach his cross. However much we attempt to "Christianize" the powers, we must not bypass preaching the gospel and calling people to embrace the reign of Christ through repentance and faith.

God intends through Christ "to reconcile to himself all things, whether things on earth or things in heaven, by making peace" (Col 1:20). God has "placed all things under his feet and appointed him to be head over everything for the church" (Eph 1:22). Through the church God intends to make known his wisdom "to the rulers and authorities in the heavenly realms" (3:10). The church is "not an end in itself but a functional outpost of God's kingdom,"[17] "a theater of God's works" (Bengel), God's display, picture window (Eph 2:7) and lighthouse (5:8) for the benefit of the world. Some of these powers deserve the loyal submission of Christians (Rom 13:1). Some of them should be Christianized by the involvement of Christians and the church in creational tasks: subjecting the resources of the world in education, politics, culture, and so on, to serve man as defined by God's intention. Some powers will be unmasked by the martyrdom of faithful believers (Rev 12:11). But Christians and the church must be under no illusion. Markus Barth says, "The power of filling, subjugating, and dominating 'all things,' including these powers is reserved to God and Christ alone. But the function of demonstrating God's dominion and love is entrusted to the church. She is appointed and equipped to be a public exponent of grace and unity. Political and social, cultural and religious forces, also all other institutions, traditions, majorities, and minorities . . . are entitled to see in their midst the beginning of a new heaven and a new earth."[18] But how?

Doing Spiritual Warfare

In view of Christ's death, Oscar Cullman compared the powers to chained beasts, kicking themselves to death. Between the resurrection and the Second Coming they are tied to a rope, still free to evince their demonic character but nevertheless bound.[19] So how are we to relate to the powers as we serve God in the world? I will try to present four options Christians have chosen as a continuum.

On one extreme some Christians view spiritual warfare exclusively as *exorcism.* They believe that intercession for society and casting out demons in individuals is the primary way Christians have of dealing with radical systemic evil. Less extreme is *the way of suffering power-lessness,* practiced by Gandhi and promoted by Anabaptist theologians. Our role is to witness, not to make changes. God himself must finally overpower the powers once and for all. Third, there is *the way of creative participation,* promoted by Richard Mouw and other Reformed theologians. The assumption here is that we are regents on earth, called to represent our King by caring for structures as well as people. Christians get into government, join action groups and take charge.

Like all service this will be difficult. On the far extreme of the continuum is *the way of revolution.* Those who promote this—sometimes under the label of liberation theology—believe that in extreme situations we have charge of our own destiny and must take charge of the historical process. Civil disobedience, such as that practiced by many who oppose abortion clinics and unjust abortion laws, is one form of this. Generally those who choose this route regard the powers as no more than social structures with no transcendent significance. In my opinion, each option has some validity. Discernment is what we most need.

Putting the Church's Mission in Context

Having done his research in the biblical theology of the powers, Pastor Marvin was in a stronger position to give guidance with the elders to the church. Mission, biblically understood, involved much more than merely protesting against a symptom of systemic evil in our society. So he encouraged the church to understand the environment in which they were serving, especially the cultural separation of intercourse and the marriage covenant. They included in their pastoral statement an assessment of some of the root causes:

Attacking the abortion problem at the clinic level is itself a partial solution. Christians must show that sexual chastity before and within marriage is not only God's way but the soundest way to personal health and satisfying sexual expression. We stand against the contemporary separation of the sexual act from the marriage covenant. We repudiate the reduction of sexual intercourse to a casual act which has no innate reproductive consequences or interpersonal responsibilities.

Christians repudiate the reasoning that an unwanted child should be eliminated, not only because there are potential parents waiting to adopt children, but because we believe that in God's sight no child is unwanted. We stand against the societal trend that the only capital offence is to be unwanted, especially during the early weeks of a mother's pregnancy.

The Christian's first challenge to the "powers" expressed in structural sin such as a law that permits the killing of the unborn, is to pray: for the lawmakers, for mothers, for those administering justice, for those willing to make a costly public statement with their minds and bodies, for those offering counselling services and homes for expectant women.

But Pastor Marvin still had a problem. Jim, his colleague, was in jail. Every week Jim sent a letter to the congregation encouraging them to be faithful to Christ, to put their lives on the line. Some of the people felt it was justified to disobey a civil law in order to obey the higher law of Jesus. Others felt Jim was a fanatic. How could Pastor Marvin encourage and uphold Jim without increasing the guilt of those who chose not to act and without alienating those who believe that civil disobedience is always wrong? This was a threat to the unity of their church. The third analogy of the nervous system helped Pastor Marvin work on this one.

The Nervous System—Fostering Unity and Obedience

Nerves are sensors and circuits for carrying messages from one part of the body to another. The nervous system is a maze of connections. The brain is the "head" of the system and is directly responsible for the control and articulation of the whole body. Equipping is a systemic process that facilitates the connection of every member to the head, in this case to Jesus. Equipping is also concerned for the interconnection of all the members, since each Christian is a "joint" (Eph 4:16 RSV). But in Pastor Marvin's fellowship different members of the church seemed to be getting different signals from the Head of the church.

Marvin had to teach on the relation of the individual Christian to civil government and the way Christians in previous generations have related to a civil government biblically when the government approved of, or promoted, a systemic evil. No pastoral statement could afford to ignore this issue.

Normally, where a government does not make idolatrous claims for itself, the Christian is called to submit to governmental authorities and to obey the law (Rom 13). There are extreme situations such as those encountered by believers addressed in the Revelation, when a government makes idolatrous claims for itself forcing believers to choose between Caesar and Christ. In these the Christian faces a most difficult vocation, one usually associated with suffering and martyrdom. Many Christians are convinced that in face of the present unjust law permitting widespread abortion, they must put their lives on the line as a sacrifice for this cause in the name of Jesus. While other Christians may not agree with their assessment, or their method, they must continue to pray for them and support them in every possible way as their consciences allow.

Civil disobedience is a difficult and desperate act for a follower of Jesus and should only be undertaken when (1) the law opposed is clearly immoral, (2) when every other possible nondisobedient resource has been exhausted, (3) when the protest is not clandestine, (4) when there is likelihood of success, and (5) when there is a willingness to pay the penalty of disobedience.[20] As Gandhi and his commentators well understood, nonviolent civil disobedience can only be an effective *political strategy* against a government that claims to be essentially Christian, and whose laws are founded on the Ten Commandments. Since this is no longer the case, and since we no longer have in Canada a social consensus based on Judaeo-Christian values we may judge the present action of the protestors facing charges of criminal contempt to be making a *witness,* rather than engaging in an effective political strategy. Whether or not they are effective in making a change we should receive their witness with gratitude and stand in solidarity with them. We should also continue to work on every available means both to *declare* our biblical perspective on the issue, and to *act* with social compassion with those who are inclined to choose the desperate act of abortion than to bring their children to full-term.

Since an equipper desires not only to help people connect with the Head for themselves, but also to strengthen mutual connections within the body, Pastor Marvin and his elders had to show how each person with a different response to the Lord may nevertheless contribute to the rich unity of the local church.

The one calling of all Christians to public discipleship (Eph 4:1) comes to each individual person differently. As Paul shows in Ephesians 4 and 1 Corinthians 12, Christian unity is attained not in spite of but because of diversity. We should therefore welcome, prize, support and depend upon all authentic Christian responses and initiatives in this grave social problem. While no single initiative may seem sufficient, the corporate whole is more than the sum of the parts. The church is the body of Christ, and not merely a collection of Christians.

So these are some of the thoughts and words Pastor Marvin and his elders spoke to the church members in the elders' pastoral statement, sermons, Sunday-school classes, private conversations and church meetings. What is not apparent from the above notes is the intensive way Pastor Marvin and his elders worked to get people in touch with the Lord for themselves without losing touch with their brother and sister. That involved reading Jim's letters from jail, praying with and for people, encouraging people to find their own path of obedience rather than to judge someone else's. This kind of relational work takes the church's nervous system seriously when equipping justice workers for society. The fourth analogy offered some help to Pastor Marvin as well.

Bone-Muscle System: Structuring for Social Justice

Bones give structure to the body. Muscles give movement. Together they contribute form and freedom. Pastor Marvin did not want to institutionalize social justice ministry but rather to provide a continuing forum for learning and doing. Remember that the equipping pastor is not the leader of the *people;* he or she is the leader of the *process.* And the process Pastor Marvin chose to give shape to this aspect of the church's mission was a curriculum on the book of Amos, used in small groups. It included practical applications in the areas of poverty, capital punishment and refugees. Another published study guide is useful: Esther Byle Bruland and Stephen Charles Mott, *A Passion for Jesus: A Passion for Justice* (Valley Forge: Judson Press, 1983).

A Structure for Developing Incarnational Mission

Using a chart borrowed from a British publication, *Mission Audit*,[21] Pastor Marvin's mission council determined that his church was in the "half-way house" (see figure 1). They had a long way to go in both social action and evangelism to become truly a church engaged in incarnational mission.

In the Christian "world" there is a subtle but significant difference between those who put evangelism first and those who put social justice first. Few have the synthesis of Professor David J. Bosch from South Africa who said, "Christianity which does not begin with the individual, does not begin; but Christianity which ends with the individual, ends."[22]

On the one hand, Dr. Samuel Escobar, South American evangelist and Christian leader says:

It is naive to affirm that all that is needed is new men in order to have a new society. Certainly every man should do whatever he is able to do to get the transforming message of Christ to his fellow citizens. But it is also true that it is precisely these new men who sometimes need to transform the structures of society so that there may be less injustice, less opportunity for man to do evil to man, for exploitation.[23]

On the other hand Donald McGavran says, "Service is good, but it must never be substituted for finding [the lost]."[24] The same polarization existed, to some degree, in Marvin's fellowship. It was a frozen polarization in a "live-and-let-live situation" with little real synthesis.

The curriculum on Amos and the one that followed on "life-style evangelism" were wonderful opportunities to work toward a more comprehensive mission philosophy that could be embraced by all the members. Evangelism and social justice are like twin blades of a scissors. Changing the image, evangelism is the center while social justice is the circumference of mission. Each depends on the other.

MISSION AUDIT

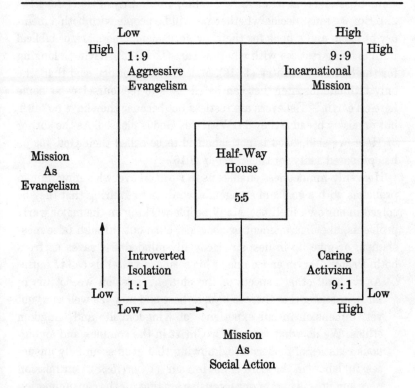

Conducting Mission with Faith and Hope

Pastor Marvin had done all he could to equip the saints in his church for justice ministry. He had taught (the digestive system). He worked with environmental issues (the circulatory system). He tried to help the people respond to the Lord's direction for themselves while living in unity with others with a different calling (the nervous system). He designed a process that would give structure to the church's movement (bone-muscle). But would it bring any lasting results? In prison, Jim wondered this about his own witness. Perhaps it would come to nothing. And Pastor Marvin wondered this, too, as he surveyed the many opportunities for justice ministry that confronted the people of his church. It helped him to locate himself in the biblical story.

We live somewhere between Eden and the New Jerusalem. We

cannot pretend that we are now dwelling in the City of God (Rev 21—22). But we must decide whether we will be people with both a memory of Eden and a hope for the New Jerusalem. One mark of biblical faith is being restless with where we are (Heb 11:9), having a longing for the heavenly country (11:16). Malcolm Muggeridge said that "the only ultimate disaster that can befall us is to feel ourselves at home here on earth."[25] Believers are restless not because they have no faith, but precisely because they do. With this God is pleased. As the author of Hebrews said, "God is not ashamed to be called their God, for he has prepared a city for them" (Heb 11:16).

Heavenly-mindedness enables us to work on overwhelming human problems with a goal and an agenda, while not requiring that they be solved in our own lifetimes. Many people working on the major world problems, like disarmament or abortion, burn out through false messianism or give up in despair. Heavenly-mindedness saves us from both. Pastor Marvin ended one of his sermons with this call to faith:

> As with all other aspects of the church's mission we do this in faith, knowing that there is both a "here and now" as well as a "not yet" dimension in our experience of Kingdom life and Kingdom ethics. We do what we can for Christ in the complex and ambiguous realities of modern life, knowing that even seemingly unsuccessful labor "in the Lord is not in vain" (1 Cor 15:58). Our mission here and now is part of our intensive longing for the consummation of the Kingdom at the second coming of Jesus.

This call to faith is echoed in a letter from Tom Merton to a young activist, apparently written to a young man during the Vietnam protest years. They could have been written by Pastor Marvin to his colleague Jim:

"Letter to a Young Activist"
February 21, 1966

Do not depend on the hope of results. When you are doing the sort of work you have taken on . . . you may have to face the fact that your work will be apparently worthless and even achieve no result at all, if not perhaps results opposite to what you expect. As you get used to this idea, you start more and more to concentrate not on the results but on the value, the rightness, the truth of the work itself. And there, too, a great deal has to be gone through, as gradually you struggle less and less for an idea and more and more for specific people. The range tends to narrow down, but it gets much more real. In the end, it is the reality of personal relationships that saves everything. . . .

It is so easy to get engrossed with ideas and slogans and myths that in the end one is left holding the bag, empty, with no trace of meaning left in it. And then the temptation is to yell louder than ever in order to make the meaning be there again by magic. . . .

The big results are not in your hands or mine, but they suddenly happen, and we can share in them; but there is no point in building our lives on this personal satisfaction, which may be denied us and which after all is not that important.

You are probably striving to build yourself an identity in your work, out of your work and your witness . . . that is not the right use of your work. All the good that you will do will come not from you but from the fact that you have allowed yourself, in the obedience of faith, to be used by God's love. Think of this more and gradually you will be free from the need to prove yourself, and you can be more open to the power that will work through you without your knowing it.

. . . If you can get free from the domination of causes and just serve Christ and truth, you will be able to do more and will be less crushed by the inevitable disappointments. Because I see nothing whatever in sight but much disappointment, frustration, and confusion. . . .

The real hope, then, is not in something we think we can do, but in God Who is making something good out of [our works] in some way we cannot see. If we can do His will, we will be helping in this process. But we will not necessarily know all about it beforehand. . . .

Enough of this. . . . It is at least a gesture. . . . I will keep you in my prayers.

      All the best, in Christ,
      Tom Merton[26]

Epilog

In this book we have explored eight examples of equipping, four in ministries when believers are together and four directed toward the release of ministry in the dispersed life of the church. I will close with a story about how the joy of equipping was brought home to me more forcefully than ever before.

Our church, Marineview Chapel, was a little bit pregnant in 1985. For several months we had been struggling with the idea of whether we were to give birth to another church. A few years before we had divided into three communities, meeting at different times in our tiny building. This story is related in chapter four of *Liberating the Laity*. Now we had filled our little building up once more to the breaking point. After several months of talking and praying about and exploring a specific building option near the university campus, we set aside a day of prayer as elders and wives. That day I got reconverted to plural leadership.

Art, one of the lay elders, started by reminding us of the vision he had when we divided into three communities: "I was cooking breakfast for me and Jessie, and I cracked three eggs, two for me and one for Jess. There they were, three yolks, but the whites all ran together. That's my church. We are still one." But that day most of us were not sure of our unity. The elders had drifted apart. As we began to deal with this, Eleanor shared a vision she had a few days before. She felt like a mother about to give birth. The Lord Jesus came to her and said exactly what we needed that day: "I see your anxious heart. I hear your anxious thoughts." But then the Lord with tender levity said, "And while I am at it, I want to give you a complete physical." This was the day the Lord gave the elders their body-life check-up! Were we healthy enough to give birth? (In case you think we are guided solely by dreams and visions let me affirm that we had done our Bible study and church-growth homework *first!* And we always test visions and prophecies by Scripture.)

Now Art had a fresh word for us. Before retirement he had been a small businessman, and one contribution he made to the eldership was to think pictorially. "When a family grows up—say parents with three children, one already married (He was thinking of how our church planted Emmanuel Christian Community in 1981.)—there is a right time for the others to leave home, not too soon *and not too late.*" I heard those last few words with all my might because Gail and I had been "chafing at the bit" to lead a group to plant a new church in a large available facility near the university campus. Sometimes, it seemed to me, the group process was too slow. Plurality was fine when it worked, but even one obstinate member could force the group to surrender, ruling by minority unless well leaned upon by one's peers, or better still well leaned upon by the Lord. I tend to be a "product" person (How can we get the job done?) rather than a process person (What is the quality of our relationship?). But that is all the more reason for a person like me to renounce the solo-pastoral role and listen to my peers. Process people need product people and vice versa. Benjamin Franklin once said that there are two things it is better not to know: what is put in sausages and how decisions are made! But I wanted to learn how to make decisions again—*together*. We had grown apart and there was rubbing. The priests in Ezekiel wore linen because their perspiration was an abomination to the Lord (Ezek 44:18). We were sweating.

We were still struggling with our diversity on the ministry of women, on styles of leadership, on the place of staff. "Dew does not come down on Mount Hermon" (Ps 133:3), and someone has added, "when the wind is blowing. We need a lot of stillness today." The Quakers distinguish between dead silence and living stillness. If you get to living stillness, plural leadership does not become minority rule. You can live with differences *if* you are in constant fellowship. "Iron sharpens iron" (Prov 27:17) when there is mutual allegiance, loyalty, sharing and burden-bearing. Seeing each other outside of elders' meetings was more important than what we did in the meeting itself. We had to keep short accounts with each other. But you can't do this from a distance. When iron is not close enough to iron to rub, it becomes an instrument to wound.

We had begun to typecast each other. We thought we knew each person's "position" on the church-plant issue. One of our elders leaned over to another and said, quite lovingly, "Are you still open to learning from this group? It seems to me your mind is made up. You have thrown down the gauntlet." Normally this would be the best time to have someone play devil's advocate. In such a big decision it is essential that someone raises *all* the reasons why it won't work, why the plan is bound to fail, why we should not do it. Mike, our chairman that day, reminded us that Eisenhower said he didn't make a decision until he found someone who disagreed with it, to point out its weakness. Mike reminded us that this is the only way to avoid "group-think," that persistent phenomenon in plural leadership where the unity breaks down *after* the decision is made because some had unspoken reservations *before* it was made. But Mike's exhortation fell on deaf ears. What we had reservations about was *ourselves*.

Then one of our elders broke down in repentance and wept. It is this supernatural dimension that makes church leadership different. We had been looking at our future options academically, clinically, descriptively and scientifically. Now we had to look at the options of the heart. This elder, who was "strong," led the way in being weak. He confessed how he saw himself as the chief hindrance to the unity of the elders' fellowship. He gave a fairly accurate statement of this and did not defend himself but cried out to God for mercy. Each of us knew that he confessed for us, and we joined him in submission to the mercy of God and wept before God. In the stillness that followed, the elders' "sweat" became as the dew of Mount Hermon, typifying our unity. Our delay had not been ungodly. It would have been carnal to go ahead against the will of some of the elders. We needed a complete physical first.

Only through the dynamics of plural leadership can we learn mutual submission with peers (as compared to submission to a superior). Each of us has a kind of Shakespearean "fatal flaw" in our personality. This is a well-documented phenomenon in business managers; it sidetracks their careers and makes them spectacular near-failures. In the church we had no hope of facing and dealing with our own "fatal flaw" alone (whether it is aggressiveness or impatience or an overwhelming need for approval). It would be tragic, according to the Ephesian definition of maturity, to build a church around one's fatal flaw because one has selected a form of eldership that minimizes personal maturity.

We need brothers and sisters who have made a covenant to be with us, who can name the lie in us and who will say nevertheless, "There is no deeper love that I have for you." But we had lost that first love. One elder leaned over to me and asked, "Is there, Paul, anyone of us with whom you would be unwilling to start a new church?" It was a searching question because I began to think of eldership as a "chosen" team rather than the team God had chosen, no matter how congenial they might seem to be. Was this to be another case of "what God has joined together let no man separate"?

Earlier in the meeting, Graeme, who uses his gift of wisdom in the elders' community, had said, "We have fished all night and caught nothing!" Now it seemed we were fishing out of the other side of the boat (Jn 21:6).

Just then Betsy returned with some pizzas and some news. While she was driving to the restaurant the Lord gave her two visions. One was of the son leaving home. He was asked to leave before he wanted to go, before they had planned to let him go. But he must go. That, she said, is how she had felt about our considerations in sending off a nucleus *until now.* (Art said, "Remember I told you, not too early, or too late.") But her second vision brought it home. She saw a mother pregnant with child. The mother didn't know how big the child would be. That was our worry. If it were three pounds it would need very special care. If it were six to eight pounds it would need less care. We resolved that together we would care for whatever God birthed among us.

What Betsy didn't immediately see is what the others realized spiritually. We were now *one* mother giving birth to *one* child. (We were in fact modern parents deciding whether we wanted to get pregnant at all. Or I should say, wondering whether we would keep the child we had!)

It was not easy for all twenty of us (ten elders and wives) to stand before each of our three congregations and to confess our sin of disunity, our experience of healing and our decision to encourage as many as were called to leave and plant a new work, University Chapel. Nor was it easy, in subsequent months, to go through the birth pangs, for there is no birthing without bruising. God had surprised us with the joy of equipping. But this time it was the equippers that got equipped!

Appendix A

How to Write an Integrated Curriculum

1. Purposes
☐ To assist the beginning student *to get into the Scripture for himself* with as few aids and helps as possible

☐ To challenge the more advanced student and older Christian to make fresh discoveries in the Bible, to challenge his pet interpretations and familiarity with the Bible

☐ To lead both to *hear* the Word of God and *do* it

2. Procedure
Your own study is the *most important* part of the process. You will undoubtedly be the one to gain the most from the whole exercise! Read the *whole book* through, more than once if possible. Note major themes, write down your discoveries as you go. Underline key phrases. Do this before you consult any helps.

Begin to study your own assigned passage intensively. Work through it word by word. Look up difficult or special words like *covenant* in a Bible dictionary. Consult Eerdman's *Handbook* for any additional introductory helps. Harrison's *Introduction to the Old Testament* and Brown's *Dictionary of New Testament Theology* are more advanced helps. Cross-reference and concordance helps will be useful. Consult a good commentary and work through the passage, making notes in your own study book. (Do not short-circuit the process by going *first* to the commentary.) Now summarize the passage using headings like the following:

a. What is the *key issue* here?

b. What are the main *sections* of the passage?

c. What areas of *our life,* individual or corporate, does this passage touch by way of application?

Preparing to Write Study Questions: Try to remember that the average person will not have done all that you have done, will not spend as long as you would wish on the exercise and might be easily frustrated by an obscure question. Ask yourself what in the passage requires *explanation* and will need an introductory note or comment.

Writing Questions for Personal Study Section: Ask the person to read the whole passage. You might sometimes direct their reading by having them note all the things they learn about, for instance, the character of God. Using your basic outline (skeleton) of the passage, start writing questions that get a person into it. Some should be *observation* questions (What, Who, Where, When). (Readers may need an occasional explanatory note to help them locate something on a map or on a time line.) Some questions should be *interpretive.* (What does it mean?) Some questions should be *application.* (What does it mean to me? What must I do about this?)

Since the curriculum is a *training tool* for people, it is important to model the principle of no application until the passage is observed and interpreted. The chart on "Understanding the Bible" on page 58 of Eerdman's *Handbook* will be of help.

Vary your style and vary *the level on which* you appeal: For example, some questions may require reflection and continued study—it may be good to say in this case, "If you are unable to answer this question now, come back to it later." Other questions could be multiple-choice options or ticking off a number on a scale of responses. (This is especially good for suggested applications.) Occasionally use a chart with fill-in sections. "Tease" a more advanced student by suggesting an optional exercise that may be a hard interpretive question, a word study, or a parallel New Testament passage (if it is in the Old Testament).

Avoid questions with yes/no or too obvious answers. But, on the other hand, avoid over-challenging questions so you will not discourage the beginning learner. Try to stay off your hobby-horse, and resist the temptation to "rig the truth" so that the person makes *your* discovery. Your questions should not leave people asking "I'm not quite sure what the writer was driving at," but rather making fresh discoveries for themselves. Make sure personal study leads to some actions to "do the doctrine."

Avoid routine, liturgical exhortations such as starting *every* personal study with "Pray for the leading of the Holy Spirit." *But* intersperse your material with encouragements such as "Stop for a moment and ask God to show you where this fits into your life."

Testing Your Study: Try the study out yourself by timing how long it takes you to do it. (It should not be more than one hour.) Then get someone who has never studied the passage to do it and to tell you what questions were vague, uncertain, irrelevant.

Writing Group Study Materials: While the study curriculum is not a guide for total group life, you may, through the group section, enhance the life of a house group by suggesting appropriate worship, fellowship dimensions, projects, and so on, that flow into or out of the study program. The group study should *assume* that everyone is doing his personal study. Approach this imaginatively not by starting each week with "share from your personal study" but building into the group study at least *one* specific contribution from personal study.

Here are some ideas:

☐ Divide the passage into sections and have each member prepared to come and share in one minute or less what they learned on that passage. In this way the whole passage can be surveyed briefly and everyone shares. This requires planning on the previous week.

Build into the personal study a specific point that will be shared with the group, such as "The one prayer request that I have for my house group as a result of studying this passage is . . ." Normally the time spent sharing from personal study should be clearly *limited in the curriculum* to the first ten to twenty minutes.

☐ Ask one member in advance to "teach" the passage from ten to fifteen minutes at the beginning of the house group meeting.

☐ An *intensive group interpretation* may focus on *one part* of the passage and explore that in-depth through further study questions.

You might assign points you were unable to explore in the personal study to two people to debate opposite interpretations, such as Romans 7 as Paul's pre-Christian experience versus Romans 7 as the struggle of a Christian. In-depth application and sharing is possible.

☐ A *group relational exercise* focuses on the application of the passage to our relationships as a group. Sometimes God is pleased to "crack a passage open to us" and give us fresh interpretation as we seek to apply it to our real life together as a house group or an assembly. The passage under study may suggest exercises that deal with some of the following relational areas:

☐ affirming one another's gifts

☐ openly communicating feelings and experiences

☐ praying for one another where we hurt and hope

☐ working through tensions in our relationships

☐ developing a Christian concept of leadership in the group that includes order, servanthood, plurality, inner authority and freedom.

Sometimes one question can get to the heart of an evening's discussion and study, such as "What would have to change in our group for us to live out the truth we have learned?"

In writing group-relational exercises you may need to spell out some guidelines, for example, "Make sure everyone shares his viewpoint on this," "Limit this part of the discussion to twenty minutes," "No one is allowed to communicate a negative thing to another in the group meeting while we are affirming strengths," "Write down all prayer requests to make sure none is ignored."

☐ A *group application exercise* explores what God is leading us to do individually or corporately as a result of our personal and group study. Usually this comes best later in the curriculum, but it may be introduced at various stages, possibly building on a previous application. In this case it is important to share and review in the group what members have heard in the passage. Then some possible areas of application may be spelled out; for example, "Which of the following areas is most challenged by this truth: home, neighborhood, community, church, work, etc."

Spell out the process of application: Are we sure God wants us to do something in this area? Pray together about it. What will it cost us to do this (time, energy, etc.)? What kind of help will we need to accomplish this? What changes will have to be made in our own life or group life to accomplish this? Be careful not to frustrate the group by *over-application,* getting them to do too many things too quickly. The editor must see that the flow of the entire curriculum leads to a balance of enjoyment, celebration, fellowship, discovery and work.

Appendix B

A Service for Commissioning Lay Pastoral Carers

Presenter: Pastor _____, the following persons have spent considerable time together learning some of the arts of the church's ministry of pastoral care: [Read the names of lay pastoral carers].

They have combined reading and discussion with visiting members and friends of this congregation to prepare for their formal recognition as lay pastoral carers.

They will continue to work together as a group to further their skills and experience in ministry, and to continue to support one another in this work.

I am pleased to present to you these men and women for commissioning as pastoral carers to minister to the homebound, the hospitalized, the institutionalized and those in special need, and to bring the consecrated elements of the holy eucharist to those who cannot join us in worship.

Pastor: One of the identifying marks of the Reformation was the reaffirmation of the priesthood or ministry of all believers. Today we are living out another chapter in that affirmation by commissioning you to assist the pastor(s) and this congregation in our ministry of pastoral care.

Already the impact of your ministry has been felt through your training, and I look forward to its continued effect. You, and the congregation, should know that the work of the pastoral carers is in addition to, not a substitute for, the pastoral care of your clergy.

I ask each of you now, having given yourself to the study and

experience of the ministry of pastoral care: Do you willingly present yourselves before God and your congregation for commissioning?
Lay Carers: We do.
Pastor: Do you pledge to the best of your ability, acknowledging the guidance of the Spirit, to seek to heal, guide, sustain and reconcile those given to your care?
Lay Carers: We do.
Pastor: Do you intend to continue your study, your growth and your support of one another in your ministry?
Lay Carers: We do.
Pastor: Will the members of _____ Church please rise. [The pastoral carers face the congregation.]

You have heard these men and women state their pledge and intention for the ministry among and with us. Do you accept them as your pastoral care assistants, and will you support their ministry with prayer, with action, with curiosity and with encouragement?
Congregation: We do so intend. [The congregation is seated and the lay pastoral carers turn to the pastor.]
Pastor: Having now heard your pledge and your intention, and having heard the support and affirmation of the members of this congregation, I joyfully commission each of you as a lay assistant into the pastoral care ministry of _____ Church. In the name of the Father, and of the Son, and of the Holy Spirit. Amen.
All: Our gracious God, you have called and you know each of us by name. Your good word to us is that you love each one of us. Bless richly, we pray, the ministry of these men and women. May a full measure of your power and your presence be their special gift, so that they might minister with joy, and caring, and gentleness and firmness.

Even as we set aside these men and women for ministry, let none of us be misled into the belief that they are doing our work. We have all been called by you. Lead us each into our special ministry.

We pray believing in your power, your love, and your presence. Amen.

This order for a service commissioning lay pastoral carers (reproduced

with minor changes) was written by the Reverend Robert W. Wohl-
fort, Ph.D., and was first used at the Lutheran Church of Saint Andrew, Silver Spring, Maryland. It may be used as is or adapted to the
needs and usage of other congregations.

Appendix C

Elders' Comments on the Ministry of the Spirit

1. The elders are aware that the Holy Spirit is freshly revitalizing the church in our area and that there have been some questions raised about our participation in some of the controversial gift ministries.

2. The elders affirm that as a church we will remain open to the full range of the ministry of the Holy Spirit as we see this witnessed in Scripture.

3. We feel that at this particular moment in the development of renewal movements in North America it is unwise completely to identify with any particular movement or leader as the final expression of the kingdom of God.

4. As we understand it, the full range of the Spirit's work amongst us includes the controversial charismata (healing, tongues, interpretation, visions, prophecy and discerning spirits), as well as the illumination of the Scripture, the work of conversion and regeneration, the unfolding of spiritual fruits, the development of Christian character, ministries of serving and witnessing and the confirmation of the love of God in the inner person.

5. We believe that the primary place for charismatic manifestations of the Spirit is within the local church and that these ministries need to be organically related to the whole life of the church.

6. In our own fellowship we expect that God the Holy Spirit will minister in many ways, including these controversial gifts, in various venues of the church's life such as prayer groups, the ministry of the elders, house groups, after-service ministry and seminars. We encour-

age this without diminishing the importance of the proclamation of the Word of God, Christian nurture, fellowship, evangelism and social justice, and worship.

7. We fully understand that there is an intrinsic awkwardness in exploring the controversial gifts. There is a necessary learning process which must take place because the charismata do not come in neat, mature packages. People will make mistakes. Love and forgiveness will be needed in the fellowship, along with correction, in order that the full benefit of the charismata can be received. We are encouraging people to explore any ministries that would edify the body or advance the kingdom. Most of us require a learning environment to take forward steps in spiritual formation. We believe that the only healthy context in which the charismatic gifts can be explored is the local church with its full range of ages and its broad experience of ministry. With God's help we will be such an environment.

8. As elders we are prepared to work with the awkwardness, to weigh, to discern and to make corrections. We would rather take this positive and biblical stance than to take a negative and overly cautious posture which would see "problems" as a threat to the life of the community.

The Elders

Appendix D

A Pastoral Letter on Prophecy Today Among Christ's People

Introduction

The intent of pastoral letters from the University Chapel eldership is to give direction to our fellowship with regard to current issues—in the world or in the church. The subject of this pastoral letter is "the gift of prophecy."

We as elders wish to clarify the manner in which we will pastor the fellowship with regard to the exercise of prophecy. Our hope is that the fellowship will be edified and Christ will be glorified.

A Commitment to Maturity in Christ

The apostle Paul valued highly the gift of prophecy for the church (1 Cor 14:1) and in all of Paul's gift lists prophecy is highlighted (Rom 12:6-8; 1 Cor 12:8-10, 28ff; 14:1-5, 6ff, 26-32; 1 Thess 5:19-22). Prophecy is one of the ministries used by the ascended Christ to nurture fellowships of Christians and the church worldwide toward maturity (Eph 4:11-13).

As elders, we rejoice with God over the resurgence of interest in and exercise of prophecy in our day. This resurgence of interest in the gift of prophecy challenges us as elders to encourage what God is doing and to guide the fellowship and those who are beginning to exercise this gift toward maturity in Christ. We realize that we cannot and should not "regulate" the work of the Spirit. Yet, biblically we are responsible to pastor and tend the flock of which God has made us overseers (1 Pet 5:2).

The following pastoral guidelines for the exercise of prophecy in a local assembly of Christians are intended to maximize the benefit of the prophetic gift and minimize the growing pains of learning to exercise a gift in a mature and edifying manner.

What Is Prophecy?

Prophecy in the New Testament teaching is one of many Spirit-inspired utterances. God reveals or brings to mind a word of encouragement, comfort or exhortation (1 Cor 14:3) to a person within the family of God who reports this word to the congregation.

The primary characteristic of prophecy is its immediacy or directness. One senses that God is speaking to his people right now with freshness. Because the primary characteristic of prophecy is immediacy, prophecy may be a spontaneous utterance (which is more difficult to test and discern), or it may be given as the result of much study, brooding, waiting, prayer and testing by trusted leaders before it is shared with the congregation. Whenever a word of true prophecy is given, it will be heard with directness.

The ministry of prophecy under the new covenant stands underneath the authority of Scripture and not alongside as an equal authority, as claimed by some word-faith teachers. Prophecy does not add any new teaching or doctrine to the Old Testament or the New Testament. Its purpose, as stated above, is to encourage, comfort and exhort. The New Testament does not support the supposed distinction that the *logos* is the Word of God in Scripture and the *rhēma* is the spontaneously spoken Word of God in prophecy.

Who May Prophesy?

According to Acts 2:17, since Christ has ascended, any believer may prophesy. It is a gift for every Christian! One would therefore expect this gift to blend with a variety of other ministries; for example, a preacher may prophesy when he or she brings the message with a Spirit-endowed directness. A person may prophesy when sharing a Scripture and making a comment, or when one shares a word of encouragement or speaks to someone one to one with a Spirit-born directness.

Two Points of Pastoral Wisdom

Given the nature of prophecy and the "supernatural" impression it makes, it easily attracts attention. Therefore it seems wise to pastor the flock in such a way that all ministries and gifts of the Spirit are honored, especially the "lesser" ones, without allowing any one gift (such as discerning of spirits or prophecy or tongues or healing) to become the trademark of our fellowship. We do not desire to be a church where one must prophesy to be "in."

Because the public meeting of the church should be marked by consistent edification in its gatherings, it seems wise that those beginning to exercise the gift of prophecy would grow, learn and mature in informal and smaller group settings.

Prophecy and the Word of Knowledge

First Corinthians 12:8 describes an utterance inspired by the Spirit called a "message of knowledge." Because of the obscurity of the Corinthian concept of "knowledge" we simply do not know definitively what this utterance was and is. At Corinth was this Spirit-inspired utterance an exposition of Christian truth (C. K. Barrett)? Or was it an expression of a prophetic ministry (either a mystery revealed or a practical word of exhortation or comfort) (Gordon Fee)? We simply do not know.

Today a phenomenon known as a "word of knowledge" is practiced, especially within the signs and wonders movement. It is fair to consider this present-day practice as a special form of prophecy since it is claimed to be a direct word from God to a person or people. Since we have no way of knowing whether this modern practice is what 1 Corinthians 12:8 describes, we must make a decision on the validity of this modern practice.

In the Old Testament and the New Testament we know of no single example where a person gives a "personal prophecy" without naming the person to whom the word is directed. We should be wary of prophecies or "words of knowledge" that describe the characteristics of a certain individual unknown to the speaker, but are nevertheless known to God and whom God is singling out for a blessing or a word or correction. We see no example of "buckshot prophecies" which are shot into a crowd in hope that the word will somehow strike the right person.

Testing a "word of knowledge" does not mean firing it off to see if someone responds. Prophecies or "words of knowledge" that are personal, especially if they are judgmental, should have the bearing "thou art the man." Examples of this are found in Ananias and Sapphira (Acts 5:1-11), Agabus and Paul (Acts 21:10-11) and Jesus with the woman by the well (Jn 4:17).

Our pastoral wisdom suggests that if a person receives a "word of knowledge," the person who receives this word should be invited to pray to the Lord that he or she might know to whom that word is directed and should approach the individual directly and privately with humility in order to ascertain whether the word is true.

"Words of knowledge" which are a medical diagnosis or a spiritual symptom of an unnamed individual or persons within the body will not be received for the reasons explained above.

Discerning Prophecy

First Thessalonians 5:19-22 exhorts us to test every reported prophecy and hold on to the good, discarding the bad without a spirit of contempt.

We offer the following three tests as the basis for discerning any reported prophecy (*Those Controversial Gifts,* Mallone p. 42ff):

1. *The theological test*
   Does this word fit with Scriptural teaching? Prophecy is not a new revelation of truth for the church, but a harmonic expression of that truth. (2 Tim 3:16-17; 1 Cor 14:37-38)
2. *The confessional test*
   Does this word originate from the Spirit of Jesus? Does this word have a scriptural balance of judgment and grace, or does it express a fleshly imbalance? (See 1 Cor 12:1-3; 1 Jn 4:1-3; Rev 19:10)
3. *The moral test*
   Does the life of the person giving the prophecy demonstrate a

submission to others in the fellowship and communion of Christ's people, and a willingness to be a servant (Mt 7:15-20; Gal 5:22-23)? As Bernard of Clairvaux said, "Learn the lesson that, if you are to do the work of a prophet, what you need is not a scepter but a hoe."

Nurturing Prophetic Gifts in Appropriate Contexts
The churches to which the apostle Paul wrote about prophecy were rarely larger than the number of people who could be accommodated in a large villa, approximately fifty. It was in this "large small group" that a person was known and there that their word was weighed by others and helpfully interpreted or corrected. It would seem pastorally wise that a small group or a larger small group be the primary context in which the prophetic gift is nurtured, encouraged and expressed. Therefore, as elders, we wish to encourage prophecy in these more informal gatherings where prayer and the seeking of God are done consistently.

Prophecy in Public Worship
Public worship constitutes a more complicated environment in which prophecy may be received and tested with integrity, for two reasons.

First, in a public gathering people will be present who are completely unknown to us and perhaps are not yet Christians. Scripture allows that unbelievers may be reached by prophecies (1 Cor 14:24), but because the experience may be very unusual for both non-Christians and young Christians, the result may be that the overall effect is unedifying.

Second, a public gathering by its very nature invites grandstanding, persons acting in a fleshly manner who desire public recognition yet do not have access through appropriate avenues of the church may find giving spontaneous words an alternative way of expressing power and persuading.

Yet, because Scripture values prophecy so highly in corporate gatherings, we want to value it as well. Therefore, it seems wise that the following pastoral practices be in effect for prophecy in the public gathering.

That All May Be Edified: Guidelines for the Exercise of Prophecy in Public Worship

1. We will teach and explain that prophecy is allowed and encouraged in the public worship service on the criteria that it be edifying and that it "fits" the public nature of the service.

2. Prophecies that are words of encouragement and upbuilding (1 Cor 14:3) may be given without checking with an elder.

3. A person who brings prophecies regularly (week after week) will be encouraged to weigh the words he or she is given in order to discern those which have special relevance for the fellowship. This sifting of wheat from chaff is not the responsibility of the congregation, but of the person who prophesies.

4. The style in which the prophecy is given is under the control of the prophet. Each prophecy should be delivered with humility. Therefore it is appropriate to begin with a phrase such as "I believe I have a message from the Lord for our encouragement" (1 Cor 14:29-32).

5. The elders will take the responsibility to discern prophecy to weigh them and, on the occasion where there is a doubtful or difficult word, to respond immediately to the congregation. This response may be cautionary, "We are not sure this is the Lord's word for us and we wish to pray about it and reflect on it"; or possibly even disciplinary, "I doubt that this is a word from the Lord but we ask you to weigh it in the next few days as we will as elders and report back to you next week."

6. The elders will not report prophecies that are received anonymously, that is, those not signed or from someone unknown to us or someone who is unwilling to be accountable to the elders.

7. Prophecies that are not only words of encouragement but have words of judgment or calls to repentance must be submitted to the elders prior to being given publicly. Any elder who receives such a word from a person in the congregation will consult with other elders and members of the congregation as appropriate to discern the word before a decision is made as to whether it is to be reported.

8. When prophecies are given publicly, the elders will undertake to report both the accuracy and fulfillment of that word to the congregation and to the person who has reported it as time passes.

Conclusion

It is our desire as elders to create an environment in which God is free to work and in which we are free to learn and grow. It is in that spirit that we have set out the guidelines above, and it is in that spirit that we are prepared to make exceptions to all of the above, realizing that God in Jesus Christ and through his Spirit, works in and through human means and wisdom, but far beyond it as well.

Toward maturity in Christ,
The Elders of University Chapel
May 1989

Appendix E

A Lay Commissioning Service

Pastor States the Following:
The ministry which you are about to begin will bring you much joy and fulfillment. At the same time it may bring into your pathway great challenges. Sometimes ministry brings with it heartaches. It is for this reason that you have entered into this moment, thoughtfully, carefully and prayerfully. You will be giving of all that God has given you. All that you possess you give to him. In a very real sense you offer yourself to God as a sacrifice. Having committed yourself to ministry in the privacy of your heart, you now make that commitment in the presence of these your brothers and sisters. By their presence, they are saying they accept the responsibility of encouraging you in your ministry. They pledge themselves to you as you commit yourself to service.

Questioning of the Candidate for Lay Ministry:
1. So you believe you have been called to ministry? "Yes, I do."
2. Do you recognize the gifts God has given you and the ways in which they can be used for his service? "Yes, I do."
3. Have you availed yourself of instruction and training which can enhance your service? "Yes, I have."
4. Are you now ready to be sent forth into your ministry by this fellowship of believers? "Yes, I am."
5. Do you desire your life to be lived in service to God and to your fellow human beings? "Yes, I do."

Questioning of the Fellowship:
Do you pledge to support those who begin new ministries? Will you
pray for them? Will you encourage them both in deeds and in words?
If so, answer, "We will."

Prayer of Consecration: (Candidates kneeling)
Father, every day with you has meaning, but this day is especially
meaningful. We come to you, committing ourselves to your service.
We are conscious of the example of the ministry of your Son Jesus.
May ours be a continuation of the work he started. Accept our activities today as a sign of our love for you and of thankfulness for what
you have done. We commit these ministers—these your people—to
you. May their ministries be fruitful. In Jesus' name. Amen.

To the Candidates:
It is a joyful task for me indeed, before God and your brothers and
sisters in Christ, to commission you to the ministry to which you have
been called.* The God who has called you will also sustain you. Amen.

* Note: You may insert the specific ministry, whether in the gathered
church such as Sunday-school teaching or in conjunction with societal vocation, such as the ministry of dentistry or to the ministry of
carpentry.

Notes

Introduction

[1]Mark Gibbs and T. Ralph Martin, *God's Frozen People; A Book for—and About—Ordinary Christians* (London: Collins-Fontana Books, 1964), p. 113.

[2]This true story was related by Kenneth Van Wyk in a lecture at Fuller Theological Seminary, Pasadena, California, January 20, 1986.

[3]Kenneth Van Wyk, *A Model for Equipping Church Laity for Ministry* (Garden Grove, Calif.: Crystal Cathedral Congregation, 1984), p. 32.

[4]John Stott uses this comparison in *Baptism and Fullness: The Work of the Holy Spirit Today* (Downers Grove, Ill.: InterVarsity Press, 1976), p. 105.

[5]Kenneth Van Wyk, *A Model*, p. 52.

[6]In *Liberating the Laity* (Downers Grove, Ill.: InterVarsity Press, 1985), pp. 109-24, I developed six aspects of the equipping task based on contextual meanings of the Greek word for equipping *(katartizō)*: (1) The equipper is a physician putting dislocated members back into correct articulation with the body. (2) The equipper is an off-duty fisherman mending, cleaning and folding his nets, getting ready for service. (3) The equipper is a stonemason, putting stones (believers) into their correct order. (4) The equipper is a potter shaping lives by the Word of God. (5) The equipper is a parent fashioning people into the image of Christ through an imitation process. (6) The equipper is a project person putting believers into right relationship with the goal of their faith.

[7]Ray Anderson, "A Theology for Ministry," in *Theological Foundations for Ministry,* ed. Ray S. Anderson (Grand Rapids, Mich.: Eerdmans, 1979), p. 8.

[8]David Watson quotes Eduard Schweizer to make the point that the *body* is more than a graphic analogy of internal relationships: "For Paul *soma* is primarily the corporeality in which man lives in this world. It is thus the *chance to meet others.* For Paul then, the Body of Christ is in the first instance the Body *given for others.*" Far from expressing mere relationality

the body is the vehicle for expressing Christ in the world today. G. Kittel, ed., *Theological Dictionary of the New Testament* (Grand Rapids, Mich.: Eerdmans, 1970), vol. 7, 1073-74.

[9]Hendrik Kraemer, *A Theology of the Laity* (Philadelphia: The Westminster Press, 1958), p. 170.

[10]Kenneth Van Wyk, *Laity Training Resource Kit* (1735 N. Maplewood, Orange County, Calif., 1984), p. 37. Also see Donald P. Smith, "Shared Ministry," *Theology Today* 36 (October 1979), pp. 338-46.

[11]Mark Gibbs and T. Ralph Martin, *God's Frozen People* (London: Fontana Books, 1964), pp. 112-14.

Chapter One: Bible Learners and Lay Preachers

[1]Søren Kierkegaard, *The Journals of Søren Kierkegaard* (London: Oxford University Press, 1959), p. 343.

[2]R. J. Peterson, "Effectiveness of Educational Techniques Compared," *Canadian Training Methods* (January-February 1972), p. 10.

[3]Virginia Satir, *Conjoint Family Therapy,* rev. ed. (Palo Alto, Calif.: Science and Behavior Books, 1983), p. 251-52.

[4]This material is substantially what was published in R. Paul Stevens, "Honing the Two-Edged Sword," *Leadership 100* (November-December, 1983), pp. 12-14.

[5]P. T. Forsyth, *Positive Preaching and the Modern Mind* (London: Independent Press Ltd., 1960), pp. 53-54.

[6]Martin Luther, "The Right and Power of a Congregation or Community to Judge All Teaching and to Call, Appoint, and Dismiss Teachers, Established and Proved from Scripture," in *Luther's Works,* ed. Helmut T. Lehmann (Philadelphia: Fortress Press, 1970), 39:310.

[7]Abbé Michonneau. *Revolution in a City Parish* (Westminster, Md.: The Newman Press, 1965), p. 131ff.

[8]Roland Bainton, *Here I Stand: A Life of Martin Luther* (New York: Mentor Books, 1950), p. 201.

[9]John R. W. Stott, *Between Two Worlds: The Art of Preaching in the Twentieth Century* (Grand Rapids: Eerdmans, 1982), pp. 180-335.

[10]George H. Williams, "The Ancient Church, AD 30-313," in *The Layman in Christian History,* ed. Stephen C. Neill and Hans-Reudi Weber (London: SCM Press, 1963), p. 41.

[11]Michael Eastman quoted in David Watson, *I Believe in Evangelism* (Grand Rapids: Eerdmans, 1979), p. 22.

Chapter Three: Lay Pastors and Caregivers

[1]Howard Clinebell, *Basic Types of Pastoral Care and Counselling* (Nashville: Abingdon Press, 1984), p. 404.

[2]Hendrik Kraemer, *Theology of the Laity* (Philadelphia: Westminster Press, 1958), p. 22.

[3]Ibid., p. 22.

[4]George H. Williams, "The Ancient Church," p. 31.

[5]Ibid.

[6]Ibid., p. 35.

[7]Ibid.

[8]Ibid., p. 40.

[9]Ibid., p. 47.

[10]Ibid.

[11]For example, Judy Schindler, "The Rise of One-Bishop-Rule in the Early Church: A Study in the Writings of Ignatius and Cyprian," in *Baptist Reformation Review* (Second Quarter 1981) 10, 2, pp. 3-9.

[12]Frend, "The Church of the Roman Empire," in *The Layman in Christian History* (London: SCM Press, 1963), p. 60.

[13]Kraemer, *Theology of the Laity,* pp. 51-52.

[14]Frend, "The Church of the Roman Empire," p. 61.

[15]Ibid., p. 62.

[16]Edwin Hatch, *The Organization of the Early Christian Churches* (New York: Burt Franklin, 1972), pp. 30-31.

[17]Frend, "Church of the Roman Empire," p. 77.

[18]Schindler, "The Rise of One-Bishop-Rule," p. 6.

[19]Rita Bennett's two books are probably the best explanation of this ministry: Rita Bennett, *You Can Be Emotionally Free* (Old Tappan, N.J.: Fleming H. Revell, 1982) and *How to Pray for Inner Healing* (Old Tappan, N.J.: Fleming H. Revell, 1984). Other books worth consulting are found in the bibliography.

[20]Quoted in Martin and Deidre Bobgan, *How to Counsel from Scripture* (Chicago: Moody Press, 1985), p. 4.

[21]Keith Gaetz, "Counselling and Spirituality" (Unpublished paper for Regent College, Vancouver, 1988), p. 1. Keith Gaetz is one of my students and has come from the experience of serving as a minister of counselling in a church. Those wishing to explore this matter further are encouraged to look at the bibliography in lay counselling.

[22]Robert R. Carkhuff, *Helping and Human Relations: A Primer for Lay and Professional Helpers* (New York: Holt, Rinehart, and Winston, 1969), vol. 1, p. 1, quoted in Clinebell, *Basic Types,* p. 397.

[23]The address of the Stephen Series is Pastoral Care Team Ministries, 7120 Lindell Blvd., St. Louis, MO 63103.

[24]Samuel Southard, *Comprehensive Pastoral Care* (Valley Forge, Pa.: Judson Press, 1975), p. 7.

[25]Adapted from a quote in Oscar Feucht, *Everyone a Minister* (St. Louis:

Concordia, 1979), p. 146.

Chapter Four: Worship Leaders and Gift-Brokers

[1]Oscar Cullmann, *Early Christian Worship,* trans. A. Stewart Todd and James Torrance (London: SCM Press, 1973) p. 29. Cullman says, "There was no gathering of the community without the breaking of bread.... The Lord's Supper is thus the basis and goal [and climax] of every gathering."

[2]Eugene H. Peterson, *Reversed Thunder: The Revelation of John and the Praying Imagination* (San Francisco: Harper & Row, 1988), p. 60.

[3]Quoted in Timothy Ware, *The Orthodox Church* (Harmondsworth, England: Penguin Books, 1988), p. 269.

[4]Joachim Jeremias, *Jerusalem in the Time of Jesus* (Philadelphia: Fortress Press, 1978), pp. 198-207. Jeremias deals with the arrangements of ordinary priests who needed to supplement the tithes by following some profession in their own district.

[5]Don and Jim in this story are collages of personalities in my home church, carefully disguised.

[6]Peter Gillquist, *The Physical Side of Being Spiritual* (Grand Rapids, Mich.: Zondervan, 1979), p. 126.

[7]George Mallone, *Furnace of Renewal* (Downers Grove, Ill.: InterVarsity Press, 1981), pp. 43-76.

[8]Some of the material in the foregoing paragraphs is adapted from my chapter "Equipping Spiritual Gifts" in George Mallone, *Those Controversial Gifts* (Downers Grove, Ill.: InterVarsity Press, 1983), pp 121-43.

[9]Leonard Doohan, *The Lay-Centred Church: Theology and Spirituality* (Minneapolis: Winston Press, 1984), p. 60.

[10]From a lecture by Elton Trueblood at McMaster Divinity College, Hamilton, Ontario, Canada 1960.

Chapter Five: Worker-Priests in the Marketplace

[1]John Redekop, "Canadian Labour: A Place for Christians?" in *Faith Today* (September-October 1989), pp. 18-23.

[2]Daniel Yankelovich, "New Rules in American Life: Searching for Self-Fulfilment in a World Turned Upside Down," *Psychology Today* April 1981, pp. 35-91 (p. 78).

[3]Christopher Lasch, *The Culture of Narcissism: American Life in an Age of Diminishing Expectations* (New York: W. W. Norton & Co., 1978), pp. 43-45. Lasch notes that the modern narcissist not only is egotistical, selfish in older terms, but is dependent on others to validate his self-esteem.

[4]Laura is not the real name of this stylized example, drawn from many case studies, explored with my students in my course "Marketplace Ministries." The other case studies mentioned are a collage of real stories with the

identities disguised.

[5]Bruce Barton, *The Man Nobody Knows* (New York: Bobbs-Merrill Co., 1924-5), p. 177.

[6]Ibid., p. 180.

[7]Denney Boyd, *The Vancouver Sun,* 15 November 1989, p. B1.

[8]Richard R. Broholm, "How Can You Believe You're a Minister When the Church Keeps Telling You You're Not?" in *The Laity in Mission,* ed. George Peck and John S. Hoffman (Valley Forge: Judson Press, 1984), pp. 21-22.

[9]Dietrich Bonhoeffer, *Life Together,* trans. John W. Doberstein (New York: Harper and Row, 1954), p. 70.

[10]Thomas Aquinas, *S. Theol.* 11-11, 187, 3, quoted in Alfons Auer, *Open to the World: An Analysis of Lay Spirituality,* trans. Dennis Doherty (Baltimore: Helican Press, 1966), p. 142.

[11]*The Poems of Robert Frost* (New York: The Modern Library, 1946), pp. 312, 314.

[12]Hendrik Kraemer, *Theology of the Laity,* p. 160.

[13]Quoted in John A. Bernbaum and Simon M. Steer, *Why Work?: Careers and Employment in Biblical Perspective* (Grand Rapids, Mich.: Baker Books, 1986), p. 21.

[14]See Dan Williams, "Was Luther's Dairy-Maid Called to Milk Cows?" in *The Equipping Bulletin,* Vancouver, B.C., vol. 1, no. 2, 3 (Fall-Winter 1986-87).

[15]William Diehl, *Thank God, It's Monday!* (Philadelphia: Fortress Press, 1982), p. 171.

[16]Ibid., p. 169.

[17]Marjorie Warkentin, *Ordination: A Biblical-Historical View* (Grand Rapids, Mich.: Eerdmans, 1982), p. 187.

[18]Wheaton, Ill.: Harold Shaw Publishers, 1989.

[19]Nelvin Vos, *Seven Days a Week: Faith in Action* (Philadelphia: Fortress Press, 1985), p. 15.

[20]Write for information to Regent College, 5800 University Blvd., Vancouver, BC V6T 2E4.

[21]MEDA can be contacted for information at either of the following addresses: 402-280 Smith St., Winnipeg, Man., Canada R3C 1K2 or P.O. Box M, Akron, PA USA 17501. They publish a useful magazine called *Marketplace.* In their official statement, they publish that business as mission can take many forms: (1) Practicing corporate shalom by ensuring that relationships, profits, products and ethics correspond with God's intention for humanity. (2) Investing in things that affirm and enhance life and refusing to invest in things that harm or diminish life. (3) Doing business in a way that supports the mission of the church. (4) Evangelism and church-planting through business. (5) Carrying out economic wholeness to the needy. (6) Doing business in problem areas of the world and there modeling the king-

dom way. (7) Using economic and political power on behalf of the powerless.

[22]Anne Rowthorn, *The Liberation of the Laity* (Wilton, Conn.: Morehouse-Barlow, 1986), p. 80.

[23]Dorothy L. Sayers, "Why Work?" in *Creed or Chaos?* (New York: Harcourt, Brace and Co., 1949), pp. 46-62.

[24]Auer, *Open to the World,* p. 230, emphasis mine.

Chapter Six: Neighborhood Evangelists
[1]*Person to Person* may be rented or purchased from P.O. Box 240, Swindon, SN5 7 HA England.

Chapter Seven: Skilled Marriage-Builders
[1]*The Poems of Robert Frost* (New York: The Modern Library, 1946), pp. 41-42.

[2]David R. Mace, *Close Companions: The Marriage Enrichment Handbook* (New York: The Continuum Publishing Co., 1982), p. 130.

[3]Kenneth Van Wyk, *A Model for Equipping Church Laity for Ministry* (Garden Grove, Calif.: Crystal Cathedral Congregation, 1981), p. 8.

[4]David and Vera Mace, *Marriage Enrichment in the Church* (Nashville: Broadman Press, 1976), pp. 61-71.

Chapter Eight: Justice-Workers in Society
[1]Pastor Marvin is a composite creation of Canadian pastors I have known who have undertaken ministry which combined evangelism and social justice.

[2]Quoted in Ronald Sider, *Rich Christians in an Age of Hunger* (Downers Grove, Ill.: InterVarsity Press, 1977), p. 58.

[3]Hendrik Kraemer, *Theology of the Laity,* p. 165.

[4]Ibid., p. 170.

[5]E. H. Oliver, *The Social Achievements of the Christian Church* (United Church of Canada, 1930), p. 84.

[6]Ibid., pp. 6-173.

[7]Ibid., p. 176.

[8]These quotes are material adapted from an article I wrote published in *Christian Week,* 12 September 1989, pp. 12-13. The pastoral problem is based on several real situations once again disguised.

[9]James Stewart, *A Faith to Proclaim* (New York: Charles Scribner's Sons, 1953), p. 66.

[10]Ibid, p. 67.

[11]Markus Barth, *Ephesians 4—6,* The Anchor Bible (Garden City, N.Y.: Doubleday, 1960), pp. 800-804, gives a helpful summary of the believer's *host* of opponents. "The 'principalities and powers' are at the same time intangible

spiritual entities and concrete historical, social, or psychic structures or institutions of all created things and all created life. They represent a certain order in God's creation—though their idolization by man has often resulted in chaotic conditions. . . . Because of the death and resurrection of the Messiah Jesus, these powers are already subject to God and Christ, and they face an even more total subjugation in the future (1 Cor 15:25-27). In the meantime, some of them deserve the saint's loyal cooperation (Rom 13:1-7; Eph 6:5-9; etc.). They are 'servants of God for the good' of man, but none of them must be idolized or worshipped. . . . Although the powers mentioned include 'death' and can eventually deserve the name of 'enemies,' not all of them are evil. Life, angels, high points of human existence or destiny are among them (Rom 8:38-39). Whether they be good or evil, they all face total subjection to the Messiah and to God at the end of the present aeon (1 Cor 15:25-27). While in Eph. 1:21, perhaps also in 2:7; 3:10, good and evil forces are listed, 6:12 speaks only of evil powers. . . . Against the corrupted structures and institutions the saints have to 'wrestle'; those powers must be 'resisted' (6:2-13). It may be asked whether the powers mentioned in Eph. 6 are the same as the demons which according to the Gospels threaten, dominate, and seek to destroy the life of individuals. An affirmative answer is suggested by the following observations: just like the powers in Eph. 6, so the demons mentioned in the Gospels are not of 'blood and flesh'; both are specifically dangerous because of their 'spiritual,' seemingly intangible, unalterable and invincible character. The distinction between the demons and powers, however, appears to be that the demons affect the individual incidentally, whereas the powers threaten all men at all times. Admittedly the two kinds of threats cannot be fully explained apart from one another. According to the insights of C. G. Jung a collective unconscious is essential to the structure of the individual psyche. Individual suffering may therefore be the result of pressures experienced by the whole human community." Barth then gives several arguments to support the interpretation, which he favors, that Ephesians 6 is addressing primarily *social* tensions and pressures.

[12]Hendrikus Berkhof, *Christ and the Powers,* trans. John Howard Yoder (Scottdale, Pa.: Herald Press, 1962), pp. 28-29.

[13]For example, Hendrikus Berkhof.

[14]As David Watson does in *The Hidden Battle* (Wheaton: Harold Shaw, 1980).

[15]Berkhof, *Christ and the Powers,* p. 39.

[16]Ibid., p. 43.

[17]Markus Barth, *Ephesians 4—6,* p. 364.

[18]Ibid., p. 365.

[19]Oscar Cullman, *Christ and Time,* p. 198, quoted in Stewart, *A Faith to*

Proclaim, p. 97.

[20]Stephen Charles Mott, *Biblical Ethics and Social Change* (New York: Oxford University Press, 1982), pp. 161, 166.

[21]*Mission Audit* (London: General Synod Board for Mission and Unity, the Church of England, 1984), p. 18.

[22]David J. Bosch, *Witness to the World* (Marshall, Morgan and Scott), p. 20, quoted in David Watson.

[23]Quoted in David Watson, *I Believe in Evangelism* (Grand Rapids, Mich.: Eerdmans, 1979), pp. 58-59.

[24]Donald A. McGavran, *Understanding Church Growth,* rev. ed. (Grand Rapids, Mich.: Eerdmans, 1980), p. 24.

[25]Malcolm Muggeridge, *Jesus Rediscovered* (London: Fontana Books, 1970), p. 17.

[26]Quoted from *The Hidden Ground of Love: The Letters of Thomas Merton on Religious Experience and Social Concerns,* ed. William H. Shannon (New York: Farrar, Straus, Giroux, 1985), pp. 294-97.

Bibliography

Chapter One: Bible Learners and Lay Preachers

Craddock, Fred B. *Preaching.* Burlington, Ont.: Welch, 1985.

Davis, H. Grady. *Design for Preaching.* Philadelphia: Fortress, 1979.

Fant, Clyde E. *Preaching for Today.* New York: Harper and Row, 1975.

Griffin, Emory. *The Mind Changers:* The Art of Christian Persuasion. Wheaton: Tyndale, 1976.

Lowry, Eugene L. *The Homiletical Plot: The Sermon As Narrative Art Form.* Atlanta: John Knox, 1980.

Pitt-Watson, Ian. *Preaching: A Kind of Folly.* Philadelphia: Westminster Press, 1976.

Robinson, Haddon W. *Biblical Preaching: The Development and Delivery of Expository Messages.* Grand Rapids, Mich.: Baker Book House, 1980.

Sangster, W. E. *The Craft of Sermon Construction.* London: The Epworth Press, 1949.

Spurgeon, Charles H. *Lectures to My Students.* London: Marshall, Morgan and Scott, 1954.

Stewart, James S. *Heralds of God.* London: Hodder and Stoughton, 1946.

Stott, John R. W. *The Preacher's Portrait.* Grand Rapids, Mich.: Eerdmans, 1961.

_____. *Between Two Worlds: The Art of Preaching in the Twentieth Century.* Grand Rapids, Mich.: Eerdmans, 1982.

Sweazey, George. *Preaching the Good News.* Englewood Cliffs: Prentice-Hall, 1976.

Thielicke, Helmut. *Life Can Begin Again: Sermons on the Sermon on the Mount.* Cambridge: James Clarke and Co., 1963.

_____. *The Waiting Father.* New York: Harper and Row, 1959.

Chapter Two: Small Group Leaders

Barker, Steve, et al. *Good Things Come in Small Groups.* Downers Grove: InterVarsity Press, 1985.

Coleman, Lyman, and Scoles, Marty. *Serendipity Training Manual for Groups.* Littleton, Co.: Serendipity, 1989.

Cosby, Gordon. *Handbook for Mission Groups.* Church of the Saviour, Washington, D.C.

Griffin, Em. *Getting Together: A Guide for Good Groups.* Downers Grove, Ill.: InterVarsity Press, 1982.

Hestenes, Roberta. *Using the Bible in Groups.* Louisville, Ky.: Westminster/John Knox, 1985.

Jensen, Irving. *Independent Bible Study.* Chicago: Moody Press, 1972.

Johnson, David W., and Johnson, Frank P. *Joining Together: Group Theory and Group Skills.* New York: Prentice-Hall, 1987.

Kunz, Marilyn, and Schell, Catherine. *How to Start a Neighborhood Bible Study.* Wheaton, Ill.: Tyndale, 1970.

Lum, Ada. *How to Begin an Evangelistic Bible Study.* Downers Grove, Ill.: InterVarsity Press, .

Nyquist, James, and Kuhatschek, Jack. *Leading Bible Discussions.* rev. ed. Downers Grove, Ill.: InterVarsity Press, 1985.

Peace, Richard. *Small Group Evangelism.* Downers Grove, Ill.: InterVarsity Press, 1983.

Snyder, Howard A. *The Radical Wesley and Patterns for Church Renewal.* Downers Grove, Ill.: InterVarsity Press, 1980.

Williams, Dan. *Seven Myths About Small Groups.* Downers Grove, Ill.: InterVarsity Press, 1991.

Chapter Three: Lay Pastors and Caregivers
1. Lay Pastoral Care

Collins, Gary. *How to Be a People Helper.* Santa Ana, Calif.: Vision House Publishers, 1976). Describes the basics of friend-to-friend helping and gives guidance on referral, help in crisis telephone help, and helping yourself.

Detwiler-Zapp, Diane, and Dixon, William C. *The Caring Church: A Guide for Lay Pastoral Care.* San Francisco: Harper & Row, 1983. The theology and methodology of lay training.

————. *Lay Caregiving.* Philadelphia: Fortress, 1982. A practical guide to lay training based on their broad experience in the Fort Wayne, Indiana, area.

Siang-Yang, Tan. *Lay Counselling: Equipping Christians for a Helping Ministry.* Grand Rapids, Mich.: Zondervan, 1991.

Steinbron, Melvin J. *Can the Pastor Do It Alone?: A Model for Preparing People for Lay Pastoring.* Ventura, Calif.: Regal, 1987.

Stone, Howard W. *The Caring Church: A Guide for Lay Pastoral Care.* San Francisco: Harper & Row, 1983.

Turley, Bruce. *Being There for Others—A Pastoral Resource for Lay People.* Melbourne, Australia: Joint Board of Christian Education of Australia and New Zealand, 1976. The principles of lay caring ministries and help in such care in specific problems—e.g., sickness, dying, bereavement, alcohol abuse, suicide.

2. Inner Healing

Bennett, Rita. *How to Pray for Inner Healing for Yourself and Others.* Old Tappan, N.J.: Fleming H. Revell, 1984.

———. *You Can Be Emotionally Free.* Old Tappan, N.J.: Fleming H. Revell, 1982.

Linn, Dennis, and Linn, Matthew. *Healing Life's Hurts: Healing Memories Through the Five Stages of Forgiveness.* New York, 1978. This work is now a type of classic. There is a lot of self-prayer included. It is based on Kübler-Ross's five stages of grief, as well as Christian imagery.

———. *Healing of Memories: Prayers and Confessions and Steps to Inner Healing.* New York: Paulist Press, 1974.

MacNutt, Francis. *Healing.* Notre Dame, Ind.: Ave Maria Pr., 1974, pp. 161-191. This book is the best source for teaching on healing in general.

Sandford, John, and Sandford, Paula. *Healing the Wounded Spirit.* South Plainfield, N.J.: Bridge Publishing, 1985.

———. *The Transformation of the Inner Man.* S. Plainfield, N.J.: Bridge Publishing Inc., 1982. This is a major integrative work, aware of psychology as well as theology. It is also from a Protestant point of view, which may make it more comfortable to some readers.

Scanlan, Michael. *Inner Healing.* New York: Paulist Press, 1974. This is one of the first books on the topic and still one of the best, especially for its size.

3. Deliverance

Green, Michael. *I Believe in Satan's Downfall.* Grand Rapids, Mich.: Wm. B. Eerdmans, 1981. This has to be the best evangelical book in the area, although it is rather general when it comes to method.

Linn, Matthew, and Linn, Dennis. *Deliverance Prayer.* New York: Paulist Press, 1981. Somewhat technical in places, but a good symposium of pastoral and psychiatric views on the topic from people who have read the literature on all sides. Catholic in orientation.

MacNutt, Francis. *Healing.* Notre Dame, Ind.: Ave Maria Press, 1974, pp. 208-231.

Scanlan, Michael, and Cirner, Randall J. *Deliverance from Evil Spirits.* Ann Arbor, Mich.: Servant Books, 1980. A careful and pastorally sensitive book by a university rector. Its important contribution is to set deliverance into the broader context of pastoral care.

Chapter Four: Worship Leaders and Gift-Brokers

Allen, Ronald, and Borror, Gordon. *Worship: Rediscovering the Missing Jewel.*

Portland: Multnomah Press, 1982.

Baillie, Donald M. *The Theology of the Sacraments.* New York: Charles Scribner's Sons, 1957.

Mallone, George. *Those Controversial Gifts.* Downers Grove, Ill.: InterVarsity Press, 1983.

Martin, Ralph P. *Worship in the Early Church.* Grand Rapids, Mich.: Eerdmans, 1964, 1974.

―――――. *The Worship of God.* Grand Rapids, Mich.: Eerdmans, 1982.

Mitchell, Robert H. *Ministry and Music.* Philadelphia: Westminster Press, 1978.

Ortlund, Anne. *Up With Worship.* Glendale: Regal Books, 1975.

Tozer, A. W. *The Knowledge of the Holy.* New York: Harper & Row, 1961.

Underhill, Evelyn. *Worship.* New York: Crossroad, 1985.

Wainwright, Geoffrey. *Doxology: A Systematic Theology.* New York: Epworth Press, 1980.

Webber, Robert E. *Worship Old & New.* Grand Rapids, Mich.: Zondervan, 1982.

―――――. *Worship Is a Verb.* Waco, Tex.: Word Books, 1985.

White, James F. *Introduction to Christian Worship.* Nashville: Abingdon, 1980.

Chapter Five: Worker-Priests in the Marketplace

1. Work

Anderson, Ray S. *Minding God's Business.* Grand Rapids, Mich.: Eerdmans, 1986.

―――――. *On Being Human: Essays in Theological Anthropology.* Grand Rapids, Mich.: Eerdmans, 1982.

Banks, Robert. *All the Business of Life: Bringing Theology Down-to-Earth.* Tring, England: Lion Publishing, 1987.

Bernbaum, John A., and Steer, Simon M. *Why Work? Careers and Employment in Biblical Perspective.* Grand Rapids, Mich.: Baker Book House, 1986.

Diehl, William E. *Thank God, It's Monday.* Philadelphia: Fortress Press, 1982.

―――――. *The Monday Connection: A Spirituality of Competence, Affirmation, and Support in the Workplace.* San Francisco: Harper & Row, 1991.

Ellul, Jacques. *Money and Power.* Downers Grove, Ill.: InterVarsity Press, 1984.

Greenleaf, Robert K. *Servant Leadership: A Journey Into the Nature of Legitimate Power and Greatness.* New York: Paulist Press, 1977.

Kraemer, Hendrik. *A Theology of the Laity.* London: Lutterworth Press, 1958.

McConnell, William T. *The Gift of Time.* Downers Grove, Ill.: InterVarsity Press, 1983.

Mattson, Ralph, and Miller, Arthur. *Finding a Job You Can Love.* Nashville: Thomas Nelson, 1982.

Mouw, Richard J. *Called to Holy Worldliness.* Philadelphia: Fortress Press, 1980.

Neill, Stephen, ed. *The Layman in Christian History.* London: SCM Press, 1963.

Peabody, Larry. *Secular Work Is a Full-Time Service.* Christian Literature Crusade, 1974.

Peck, George, and Hoffman, John D., eds. *The Laity in Ministry.* Valley Forge: Judson, 1984.

Pountney, Michael. *Getting a Job: A Guide for Choosing a Career.* Downers Grove, Ill.: InterVarsity Press, 1984.

Schoberg, Gerry, and Stevens, R. Paul. *Satisfying Work: Christian Living from Nine to Five.* Wheaton, Ill.: Harold Shaw Publishers, 1989.

Slocum, Robert E. *Ordinary Christians in a High-Tech World.* Waco, Tex.: Word Books, 1986.

Stevens, Paul. *Liberating the Laity.* Downers Grove, Ill.: InterVarsity Press, 1985.

Stott, John. *One People.* Old Tappan, N.J.: Fleming H. Revell, 1982.

Tucker, Graham. *The Faith-Work Connection: A Practical Application of Christian Values in the Marketplace.* Toronto: Anglican Book Centre, 1987.

———. *It's Your Life: Create a Christian Lifestyle.* Toronto: Anglican Book Centre, 1977.

2. Ethical Decision-Making

Kraemer, Hendrik. *The Bible and Social Ethics.* Social Ethics Series 5, Philadelphia: Fortress Press, 1956.

Long, Edward. *Conscience and Compromise.* Philadelphia: Westminster Press, 1954.

Longenecker, Richard. *New Testament Social Ethics for Today.* Grand Rapids, Mich.: Eerdmans, 1984.

Mott, Stephen Charles. *Biblical Ethics and Social Change.* New York: Oxford University Press, 1982.

Ramsey, Paul. *Basic Christian Ethics.* Chicago: University of Chicago Press, 1977.

Smedes, Lewis. *Mere Morality: What God Expects of Ordinary People.* Grand Rapids, Mich.: Eerdmans, 1983.

Chapter Six: Neighborhood Evangelists

Coleman, Robert. *The Master Plan of Evangelism.* Westwood, N.J.: Fleming H. Revell, 1964.

Green, Michael. *Evangelism in the Early Church*. London: Hodder and Stoughton, 1970.

―――. *Evangelism Through the Local Church*. London: Hodder and Stoughton, 1990.

―――. *Freed to Serve: Training and Equipping for Ministry*. Dallas: Word, 1983.

―――. *Why Bother with Jesus?* London: Hodder and Stoughton, 1979.

Groothuis, Douglas. *Confronting the New Age*. Downers Grove, Ill.: InterVarsity Press, 1988.

Kirk, Andrew. *The Good News of the Coming Kingdom: The Marriage of Evangelism and Social Responsibility*. Downers Grove, Ill. InterVarsity Press, 1983.

Little, Paul. *How to Give Away Your Faith*. Downers Grove, Ill.: InterVarsity Press, 1966.

Pinnock, Clark. *Reason Enough: A Case for the Christian Faith*. Downers Grove, Ill.: InterVarsity Press, 1980.

Pippert, Rebecca Manley. *Out of the Saltshaker*. Downers Grove, Ill.: InterVarsity Press, 1980.

Posterski, Don. *Reinventing Evangelism*. Downers Grove, Ill.: InterVarsity Press, 1989.

Watson, David. *I Believe in Evangelism*. Grand Rapids, Mich.: Eerdmans, 1979.

Chapter Seven: Skilled Marriage Builders

1. Theology of Marriage

Anderson, Ray S. *On Being Human: Essays in Theological Anthropology*. Grand Rapids, Mich.: Eerdmans, 1982.

Anderson, Ray S., and Guernsey, Dennis B. *On Being Family: A Social Theology of the Family*. Grand Rapids, Mich.: Eerdmans, 1985.

Barth, Karl. *On Marriage*. Philadelphia: Fortress Press, 1968.

Bromiley, Geoffrey. *God and Marriage*. Grand Rapids, Mich.: Eerdmans, 1980.

Forsyth, P. T. *Marriage: Its Ethic and Religion*. London: Hodder and Stoughton, n.d.

2. Sociology and Psychology of Marriage

Baker, Maureen, ed. *The Family: Changing Trends in Canada*. Toronto: McGraw Hill Ryerson, 1984.

Berger, Brigitte, and Berger, Peter L. *The War Over the Family: Capturing the Middle Ground*. Garden City, N.Y.: Anchor Books, 1983.

Friedman, Edwin H. *Generation to Generation: Family Process in Church and Synagogue*. Gilford Press, 1985.

Galvin, Kathleen, and Brommel, Bernard. *Family Communication: Cohesion and Change.* Scott, Foresman and Co., 1982.

Lerer, William, and Jackson, Don. *The Mirages of Marriage.* New York: Norton, 1968.

Satir, Virginia. *Conjoint Family Therapy.* Palo Alto, Calif.: Science and Behavior Books, 1964.

3. Spirituality of Marriage

Leckey, Dolores. *The Ordinary Way: A Family Spirituality.* New York: Crossroads, 1982.

Mason, Mike. *The Mystery of Marriage.* Portland, Oreg.: Multnomah, 1985.

O'Brien, Gene, and Tate O'Brien, Judith. *Couples Praying: A Special Intimacy.* New York: Paulist Press, 1986.

Stevens, R. Paul. *Marriage Spirituality.* Downers Grove, Ill: InterVarsity Press, 1989.

4. Marriage Ministry

Clinebell, Howard, and Clinebell, Charlotte. *The Intimate Marriage.* New York: Harper and Row, 1970.

Garland, Diana S. Richmond. *Working with Couples for Marriage Enrichment.* San Francisco: S. F. Jossey-Bass, 1983.

Guernsey, Dennis B. *A New Design for Family Ministry.* Elgin, Ill.: David C. Cook, 1981.

Gundry, Patricia. *Heirs Together.* Grand Rapids, Mich.: Zondervan, 1980.

Huggett, Joyce. *Creative Conflict: How to Confront and Stay Friends.* Downers Grove, Ill.: InterVarsity Press, 1984.

Mace, David R. *Close Companions.* New York: Continuum Press Co., 1982.

Mace, David, and Mace, Vera. *We Can Have Better Marriages.* Nashville: Abingdon Press, 1974.

———. *What's Happening to Clergy Marriages?* Nashville: Abingdon Press, 1980.

Sell, Charles M. *Family Ministry: Enrichment of Family Life Through the Church.* Grand Rapids, Mich.: Zondervan, 1981.

Stevens, R. Paul. *Married for Good: The Lost Art of Remaining Happily Married.* Downers Grove, Ill.: InterVarsity Press, 1986.

Swindoll, Charles R. *Strike the Original Match.* Portland, Oreg.: Multnomah Press, 1980.

Tournier, Paul. *The Gift of Feeling.* Louisville, Ky.: Westminster/John Knox, 1981.

———. *To Understand Each Other.* Old Tappan, N.J.: Fleming H. Revell, 1967.

Wheat, Ed. *Love Life: For Every Married Couple.* Grand Rapids, Mich.: Zondervan, 1980.

Whitehead, James, and Whitehead, Evelyn. *Marrying Well.* New York: Doubleday, 1983.

Wright, Norman H. *Seasons of a Marriage.* Ventura, Calif.: Regal Books, 1982.

5. Premarital

Huggett, Joyce. *Dating, Sex and Friendship.* Downers Grove, Ill.: InterVarsity Press, 1985.

Short, Ray E. *Sex, Love or Infatuation: How Can I Really Know?* Minneapolis: Augsburg, 1978.

Stevens, R. Paul. *Getting Ready for a Great Marriage.* Colorado Springs: NavPress, 1990.

Wright, Norman H. *Premarital Counselling: A Guide Book for the Counsellor.* rev. ed. Chicago: Moody Press, 1982.

Wright, Norman, and Immon, Marvin. *Dating, Waiting and Choosing a Mate: A Guidebook.* Eugene, Oreg.: Harvest House, 1978.

6. Sexuality

Penner, Clifford, and Penner, Joyce. *The Gift of Sex.* Waco, Tex.: Word Books, 1981.

Smedes, Lewis B. *Sex for Christians.* Grand Rapids, Mich.: Eerdmans, 1976.

White, John. *Eros Defiled: The Christian and Sexual Sin.* Downers Grove, Ill.: InterVarsity Press, 1977.

7. Study Guides

Reapsome, James, and Reapsome, Martha. *Marriage: God's Design in Intimacy.* Lifebuilder Bible Studies. Downer's Grove: InterVarsity Press, 1986.

Roberts, Wes; Roberts, Judy; and Wright, Norman H. *After You Say 'I Do': A Marriage Manual for Couples.* Eugene, Oreg.: Harvest House, 1979.

Roberts, Wes, and Wright, Norman H. *Before You Say 'I Do'.* Eugene, Oreg.: Harvest House, 1978.

Fryling, Alice, and Fryling, Robert. *A Handbook for Engaged Couples.* Downers Grove, Ill.: InterVarsity Press, 1977.

Stevens, Gail, and Stevens, R. Paul. *Marriage: Learning from Couples in Scripture.* Wheaton, Ill.: Harold Shaw, 1991.

8. Divorce

Askin, Edith, and Rubin, Estelle. *Part-Time Father.* New York: The Vanguard Press, Inc., 1976.

Atkinson, David. *To Have and to Hold: The Marriage Covenant and the Discipline of Divorce.* Grand Rapids, Mich.: Eerdmans, 1979.

Duncan, T. Roger, and Duncan, Darlene. *You're Divorced, But Your Children Aren't.* Englewood Cliffs, N.J.: Prentice-Hall, Inc. 1979.

Duty, Guy. *Divorce and Remarriage.* Minneapolis: Bethany Press, 1967.

Gardner, Richard. *A Boys' and Girls' Book about Divorce.* New York: Bantam, 1971.

Grollman, Earl A. *Explaining Divorce to Children.* Boston: Beacon Press, 1968.

Heth, William A., and Wenham, Gordon J. *Jesus and Divorce.* London: Hodder and Stoughton, 1984.

Jewett, Claudia L. *Helping Children Cope with Separation and Loss.* Harvard, Mass.: The Harvard Common Press, 1982.

Small, Dwight Hervey. *The Right to Remarry.* Old Tappan, N.J.: Fleming H. Revell, 1975.

Smedes, Lewis B. *Forgive and Forget.* San Francisco: Harper & Row Publishers, 1984.

Steinzor, Bernard. *When Parents Divorce.* New York: Pantheon Books, 1969.

Chapter Eight: Justice-Workers in Society

Berger, Peter. *The Sacred Canopy: Elements of a Sociological Theology of Religion.* Garden City, N.Y.: Doubleday & Co., 1969.

Berkhof, Hendrik. *Christ and the Powers.* Translated by John Yoder. Scottdale, Pa.: Herald Press, 1962.

Bruland, Esther Byle, and Mott, Stephen Charles. *A Passion for Jesus; A Passion for Justice.* Valley Forge, Pa.: Judson Press, 1983.

Cosby, Gordon. *Handbook for Mission Groups.* D.C.: Church of the Savior, n.d.

Cullmann, Oscar. *Christ and Time: The Primitive Christian Conception of Time and History.* Translated by Floyd V. Filson. London: SCM Press, 1951.

Green, Michael. *I Believe in Satan's Downfall.* London: Hodder and Stoughton, 1981.

Kraemer, Hendrik. *The Bible and Social Ethics.* Social Ethics Series 5. Philadelphia: Fortress Press, 1965.

Longenecker, Richard. *New Testament Social Ethics for Today.* Grand Rapids, Mich.: Eerdmans, 1984.

Marshall, Paul. *Thine Is the Kingdom: A Biblical Perspective on the Nature of Government and Politics Today.* Hants, U.K.: Marshall, Morgan and Scott, 1984.

Mott, Stephen Charles. *Biblical Ethics and Social Change.* New York: Oxford University Press, 1982.

Ramsey, Paul. *Basic Christian Ethics.* Chicago: University of Chicago Press, 1977.

Sider, Ronald J. *Rich Christians in an Age of Hunger.* Downers Grove, Ill.: InterVarsity Press, 1977.

Sine, Tom. *The Mustard Seed Conspiracy.* Waco, Tex.: Word Books, 1981.

Smedes, Lewis. *Mere Morality: What God Expects of Ordinary People.* Grand Rapids, Mich.: Eerdmans, 1983.

Snyder, Howard A. *Liberating the Church.* Downers Grove, Ill.: InterVarsity Press, 1983.

Stringfellow, William. *An Ethic for Christians and Other Aliens in a Strange Land.* Waco, Tex.: Word Books, 1973.

Watson, David. *Called and Committed: World-Changing Discipleship,* Wheaton, Ill.: Harold Shaw, 1982.

————. *The Hidden Battle: Strategies for Spiritual Victory.* Wheaton, Ill.: Harold Shaw, 1980.

Wink, Walter. *Naming the Powers: The Language of Power in the New Testament.* Philadelphia: Fortress Press, 1984.

————. *Unmasking the Powers: The Invisible Forces that Determine Human Existence.* Philadelphia: Fortress Press, 1986.

Yoder, John H. *The Politics of Jesus.* Grand Rapids, Mich.: Eerdmans, 1972.

253
ST845

LINCOLN CHRISTIAN COLLEGE AND SEMINARY 8613

253   Stevens, R. Paul,
ST845   The equipper's
        guide to
        every-member
        ministry   86134

DEMCO